Contents

Introduction

He'd said they couldn't afford to kill him; without him they'd never find the money. If the American government found him first, they'd take him back to the US. If the others found him, they'd torture him until he told them where the money was.

Patrick Lanigan died in a car crash. Then, six weeks after his "death," his partners realized that he was still alive. He had also stolen ninety million dollars from them and their client. The search for Patrick began.

Now, four years later, he's been found. How was he found? How did he steal the money? Will the partners and their client ever recover it?

John Grisham began his career as lawyer in Mississippi. He was also a politician who wanted to make a difference in the world. His first novel, *A Time to Kill* (1989), was so successful that he continued writing legal adventure novels: *The Firm* (1991), *The Pelican Brief* (1992), *The Client* (1993), *The Chamber* (1994), *The Rainmaker* (1995), *The Runaway Jury* (1996), *The Partner* (1997), *The Street Lawyer* (1998), *The Testament* (1999) and *The Brethren* (2000). Many of his books are about serious legal topics, like the responsibilities of tobacco companies, the death penalty, the behavior of medical insurance companies, and treatment of the homeless. All have been very popular, and millions of copies have been sold around the world.

Several of Grisham's novels have been made into movies. They are all available as Penguin Readers.

Chapter 1   Ponta Pora, Brazil

They found him in Ponta Pora, a pleasant little town in Brazil, on the border of Paraguay. He lived alone in a small house on Rua Tiradentes and drove a red 1983 Volkswagen. He was thinner. His skin and hair were darker, and his nose and chin were different.

They considered taking him quickly but decided to wait. When he went downtown, they followed him and took photos. They listened as he talked to a clerk in the market. His Portuguese was excellent, almost without an accent. They watched as he ran along Rua Tiradentes and into the countryside. He was serious about his running, and this pleased them. Danilo would simply run into their arms.

♦

Guy was from Washington, DC, and had been hired to find Danilo. He'd been searching for him for four years and had spent 3.5 million dollars, all for nothing. But now he'd found him.

Osmar and his Brazilian friends didn't know why Guy wanted Danilo, but they guessed that he'd disappeared and taken a lot of money. They made large copies of the photos and put them on the wall of the small house they were staying in. They studied them carefully. Was it really him?

Osmar wanted to take him now, but Guy said they'd wait. Then, on the fourth day, Danilo raced to the airport, parked his car, got on a small plane to São Paulo, and was gone.

They waited, watching the red Volkswagen and the arriving planes. Osmar was confident that Danilo would return and they'd get him. He returned on the fifth day, and everyone was happy.

♦

Every day, Danilo ran his 10-kilometer course, leaving at almost the same time. On the eighth day, when Danilo came over the top of a hill, a small car with a flat tire was blocking the road. Its trunk was open. The young driver pretended to be surprised at the sight of the thin runner.

"*Bom dia*,"★ the young man said, stepping toward Danilo.

"*Bom dia*," Danilo said, approaching the car.

The driver suddenly took a large gun from the trunk and pointed it at Danilo's face. Danilo stopped, his eyes staring at the gun, his mouth open with heavy breathing. The driver quickly put his hands around Danilo's neck, pulled him roughly toward the car, and pushed him into the trunk. Danilo struggled and kicked, but with no effect.

The driver shut the trunk and drove to meet his friends. They took Danilo out, tied ropes around his wrists, and covered his eyes with a black cloth. Then they pushed him into the back of a van.

"What do you want?" he asked, in Portuguese.

"Don't speak," Osmar replied, in English. The Brazilian sitting on Danilo's left took a needle out of a box, filled it with a liquid, and pushed it hard into Danilo's upper arm. Danilo relaxed as the drug entered his body. His eyes closed.

They hid him under some boxes filled with fruit and drove across the border into Paraguay. An hour after the kidnapping, they turned down a dirt road and stopped at a small house that couldn't be seen from the road. They carried him inside and put him on a table. Guy and another man took his fingerprints while he slept, and compared them with the prints of a lawyer named Patrick.

"It's him," the fingerprint man said in English. They actually clapped.

Guy was excited when he made his daily call to Washington. He smiled as he said, "It's him. The prints are a perfect match."

★ *Bom dia*: "Good day," in Portuguese.

2

There was a pause, and then the other person asked, "What about the money?"

Guy was sure he'd find it. "We haven't started yet. He's still drugged."

"Call me," Stephano said.

◆

The man used Danilo's keys to open the door to his house. He collected all the computer disks. He went through the files on the desk but couldn't find what he was looking for.

Five minutes after the door opened, a silent signal was sent and a phone call was made. It informed the person on the other end that the house had been entered by a stranger. The directions in the guard's file were clear: do not call the police; call a number in Rio and ask for Eva Miranda.

◆

Eva put the phone down. The message meant that Danilo was missing. She told herself to relax. She'd need to be calm to do what she had to do. She took a file from a locked drawer and read the sheet of instructions again.

Danilo's instructions were general. The details were left to her. *She* divided the money. She'd made the list of imaginary companies in which the money was hidden; Danilo had never seen her list. As a lawyer, she worked with international businessmen and understood foreign money and banking. She knew how to move money around the world, and Danilo had taught her more.

At the moment, the money was in two places: a bank in Panama and one in Bermuda. Because European banks were closed now, she'd keep the money in the Caribbean for a few hours. She faxed instructions to move it out of Panama and Bermuda and into banks on Grand Cayman and in the Bahamas.

As time passed and there was no phone call from Danilo, she became more concerned. He wouldn't disappear without telling her first. But if they'd found him, they wouldn't wait long before they tried to make him talk. That was what he feared the most. That was why she had to run.

She went to a pay phone in the entrance of her office building and called the office of the FBI★ in Biloxi, Mississippi, asking for Agent Joshua Cutter. When he came to the phone, she asked, "Are you in charge of the Patrick Lanigan investigation?" She knew he was.

There was a pause. Then he said, "Yes. Who is this?"

"I'm calling from Brazil," she said. "They've captured Patrick."

"Who has?"

"Jack Stephano, a private detective in Washington," she answered. "He's been searching for Patrick for four years."

"And you say he's found him. Where? When?"

"Here. In Brazil. Today. And I think they might kill him."

Cutter paused. "What else can you tell me?" he asked.

She gave him Jack Stephano's phone number in Washington. Then she put the phone down and left the building. She took a taxi to the airport and flew to Curitiba.

◆

Two FBI agents entered Stephano's office.

"What are you doing here?" Stephano demanded.

"Who hired you to find Patrick Lanigan?" asked Agent One.

"I can't tell you that," Stephano answered.

"We got a call from Brazil this afternoon," said Agent Two.

Stephano had also had a call from Brazil—from Guy. He tried to seem unconcerned as he wondered who had contacted the

---

★ FBI: the FBI investigates matters that concern the American government.

4

FBI. He knew he could depend on Guy. Guy would never talk to anyone, especially the FBI.

"Where's Patrick?" Agent One asked.

"Maybe he's in Brazil."

"He belongs to us," said Agent One.

"We want him," demanded Agent Two. "Now."

"I can't help you," Stephano said.

"You're lying," said Agent One.

Agent Two said, "We have men downstairs, outside, around the corner, and outside your home. We'll watch every move you make from now until we get Lanigan."

"That's fine. You can leave now."

"And don't hurt him, OK? If anything happens to him, you'll regret it," Agent One said, and they left.

Stephano was confused. He'd spent a lot of time and money making certain that no one knew what he was doing. He'd never been caught before. No one ever knew who Stephano was following.

Chapter 2 Paraguay

Danilo was lying on a board with holes in it. Ropes through the holes and around his ankles, knees, waist, chest, and wrists held him tightly against it. A Brazilian doctor stepped into the room and pushed a needle into his arm. The drug ran into Danilo's body.

Guy entered the room alone. "Hello, Patrick," he said.

Danilo knew that his quiet life on Rua Tiradentes was finished. He wasn't Danilo Silva now; he was Patrick again. For four years, he'd wondered how he'd feel if they caught him. Now he knew. He was extremely frightened.

"Can you hear me, Patrick?" Guy asked. "We know who you

5

are. You're Patrick Lanigan from Biloxi, Mississippi. You're a lawyer. You have a wife and a daughter, age six. You've been missing now for over four years."

"That's me."

"Tell me, Patrick, did you watch your own funeral?"

"Yes. I watched it."

"Where did you hide after your funeral?"

"Here and there."

"Where's the money, Patrick?" Guy asked with a smile.

"What money?"

"The money you took with you."

"Oh, that money," Patrick said. Then he lost consciousness.

More men entered the room. They cut his clothes off and shaved several parts of his body. Then they taped small metal plates to the shaved skin. Wires connected to the metal went across his body to a box in Guy's hand.

Patrick told himself that they weren't going to kill him. He'd imagined this situation a thousand times and prayed it would never happen. But he'd always known it would. He always knew they were out there, searching for him.

He closed his eyes, tried to breathe regularly, and struggled to control his thoughts. "I don't know where the money is. I don't know where the money is," he repeated silently.

Until today, he'd called Eva every day between 4 P.M. and 6 P.M., so he knew that she'd moved the money by now—that it was safely hidden. He didn't know where it was. But would they believe him?

The doctor returned and pushed another needle into his arm. "Where's the money, Patrick?" Guy asked.

"I don't have any money," Patrick replied.

"You *will* tell me, Patrick. You can do it now, or you can do it ten hours from now when you're half-dead."

"I don't want to die, OK?" Patrick said, his eyes filled with fear. "They won't kill me," he told himself.

Guy held the box close to Patrick's face. "See this?" he said. "When I push this lever, electricity will pass through the wires to the metal plates on your skin. Now, where's the money?"

"I don't know. I swear."

Guy pushed the lever and electricity shot through Patrick's body, burning his skin. He closed his eyes and mouth tightly, making an effort not to scream. But he stopped trying after a second and screamed loudly.

"Tell me where the money is, and you'll leave this room alive. We'll take you back to Ponta Pora. We won't tell the FBI." Guy paused. "If, however, you refuse to tell me where the money is, then you'll never leave this room alive. Do you understand, Patrick?"

"Yes. I swear I don't know. If I knew, I'd tell you." Guy pushed the lever down. "I don't know!" Patrick screamed in pain. "I swear I don't know."

Guy waited a few seconds for Patrick to recover. Then he asked calmly, "Where's the money?"

"I don't know!" Patrick's screams filled the house.

They left him alone for a few minutes to suffer and think about what would happen next. His skin was red from the heat and electricity. Blood ran from under the tape on his chest, where the metal was burning into his flesh. The ropes around his wrists and ankles had rubbed away his skin.

Then Guy returned alone and sat on a chair next to Patrick. "Where were you during the funeral?" he asked.

Patrick relaxed a little. Finally, there was a question that wasn't about money. Maybe if he cooperated, they wouldn't torture him again.

"I was hiding in Biloxi," he said.

"Of course. And you watched your own funeral."

"Yes. I was in a tree."

"Where did you go after the funeral?" Guy asked.

"To Mobile, Alabama."

"You changed your appearance."

"Yes. I shaved my beard, colored my hair, and lost thirty kilos," Patrick explained.

"Did you study a language?"

"I studied Portuguese."

"So, you knew you were coming to Brazil."

"Yes. I thought Brazil would be a good place to hide."

"You became Danilo Silva," Guy said.

"Yes."

"And you went to São Paulo. Tell me what you did there."

"There are twenty million people there. A wonderful place to hide. I hired a teacher and learned to speak Portuguese very well. I lost more weight. I moved a lot."

"What did you do with the money?"

Patrick paused. Why did they have to keep asking about the money? "What money?" he asked.

"The ninety million dollars you stole from your law firm and its client."

"I told you. You have the wrong guy."

Guy shouted and the other Americans rushed in. The Brazilian doctor pushed another needle roughly into Patrick's arm and left. The tape recorder was turned on. Guy stood, ready to move the lever if Patrick didn't talk.

"The money arrived by wire to your law firm's bank account in Nassau on March 26, 1992—forty-five days after your "death." You were there, Patrick, pretending to be someone else. We have photos taken by the bank's hidden camera. A short time after the money arrived, it was gone—sent by wire to a bank in Malta. You stole it, Patrick. Now, where is it? Tell me, and you'll live."

Patrick looked at Guy, then at the lever, and closed his eyes tightly. "I swear I don't know what you're talking about," he said.

"Patrick, Patrick—" Guy pushed the lever down. Patrick's scream was so loud and terrible that Osmar and the Brazilians in the yard stopped their conversation. A hundred meters away, a Brazilian guarding the house offered a prayer.

♦

The apartment in Curitiba was near the airport. Eva told the taxi driver to wait while she went inside. She knew exactly what to do. She went to the locked file cabinet, opened the three drawers, took out the financial records, and put them in a suitcase to take with her. Danilo couldn't know where his papers were. Then she quickly left and was driven to a small hotel downtown.

In her room she unpacked her small fax machine and connected it to the phone line. The Asian and Zurich banks were open now. Soon the bed was covered with sheets of instructions to move the money.

She was tired, but she couldn't sleep. Danilo had said they'd come looking for her. She couldn't go home. Her thoughts weren't on money, but on him. Was he alive? If so, how much was he suffering? How much had he told them? She wiped her eyes and began to arrange the papers. There was no time for tears.

In the morning, Eva called her father. He knew from her voice that something was wrong, but she said she was safe. A client in Europe suddenly needed her for two weeks. Next, she called her law firm partner and her secretary, telling them she was needed in Germany immediately.

Eva thought about the many possibilities they'd discussed. Maybe Danilo was still alive somewhere. He'd said they couldn't afford to kill him; without him they'd never find the money. If the American government found him first, they'd take him back to the US. If the others found him, they'd torture him until he

9

told them where the money was. Maybe he'd talked; maybe he'd mentioned her name.

She flew to Buenos Aires. Then she got out her new passport, the one Danilo had helped her get a year ago. She was Leah Pires now. From Buenos Aires she flew to New York and then to Zurich.

Chapter 3   Return to North America

Mrs. Stephano was going crazy. Several neighbors had called about the FBI agents parked in front of their house. She didn't care what her husband did at the office. She did, however, care a lot about what the neighbors might think.

She went to bed at midnight. At 3 A.M. the doorbell rang, and Jack, who had fallen asleep on the sofa, answered it. Four agents were there, and he quickly recognized Hamilton Jaynes, Assistant Director of the FBI.

The men went to Stephano's living room and sat down. Jaynes said, "We're working on the Lanigan case. We've been informed that your people have him. Is this true?"

"No." Stephano remained calm.

"I'm prepared to arrest you."

"What for?" Stephano asked.

"Hiding a person wanted by the government. Lack of cooperation with the government's investigation. We'll include anything we need to. I just want to put you in jail; then we'll arrest the rest of your firm and your clients. We'll take care of the indictments later, depending on whether or not we get Lanigan. Do you understand?"

"Yes. I think so."

"Where's Lanigan?" Jaynes asked. "I want him. Now."

Stephano thought for a moment. In these circumstances,

cooperation sounded like good idea. If Patrick was given a choice of life in prison, he might make the money appear. "All right. Give me twenty-four hours, and I'll give you Lanigan. And you stop threatening to arrest me."

"Agreed. I need to know where to pick him up."

"Send a plane to Asunción, Paraguay."

"He'd better be OK. If he has any marks on his body, you'll be responsible."

Jaynes and his agents left. Stephano called Guy. "Is he talking? What do you know?" he asked.

"A little. The money still exists. He doesn't know where it is. It's controlled by a woman in Rio, a lawyer. Osmar's people in Rio are looking for her now."

"Stop whatever you're doing," Stephano instructed. "Get the doctor to take care of him and make him look good. Drive him to Asunción as soon as possible. The FBI knows about us. Make sure he's not hurt."

"Not hurt? I've been trying to kill him for five hours."

"Just do as I say. And find the woman."

Guy told the men to give Patrick some water. They cut the ropes from his wrists and ankles and removed the wires, tape, and metal plates. The doctor treated the burns on his body and gave him drugs for the pain. Then they took him to the van, laid him on the back seat, and drove to the airport in Asunción.

The next morning, they put him on a plane, and an Air Force doctor took possession of the prisoner. When the plane arrived at a Navy base outside San Juan, Puerto Rico, Patrick was taken to the base hospital. After almost four and a half years, he was back on US land.

◆

Jack Stephano was arrested by the FBI in his Washington office and taken to Jaynes's office. He swore Patrick had told them nothing about the money. When he was released, he went to a hotel and called Benny Aricia, the client whose ninety million dollars had been stolen. Sixty million dollars of that money was his; the other thirty million was for his lawyers—Bogan, Vitrano, and their partners in Patrick's old law firm. But the money had disappeared before it reached Aricia's account.

An hour later, Aricia and Stephano met at another hotel. "Am I going to be arrested?" Aricia asked.

"Probably not, but be careful."

"Have you found the girl yet?"

"Not yet. Our people in Rio found her father, but he wouldn't talk. Neither would her law firm. She's out of town on business, they say."

"What exactly did Patrick say?" Aricia asked.

"I haven't heard the tape yet," Stephano replied. "But according to Guy, he talked after five hours of torture. He said the money was all still there, hidden in various banks, but he doesn't know which banks. The girl has control of the money. He told us her name. Guy's men immediately called Rio, but she'd already disappeared."

Chapter 4   Biloxi

Since Patrick's disappearance, the remaining four partners in his law firm had had problems. They drank too much alcohol and argued a lot. They'd buried Patrick on February 11, 1992. But six weeks later, he somehow stole their money—money they'd already spent on new homes, big boats, and vacation houses in the Caribbean. Now they were desperate to get their money back.

Bogan and Vitrano were at their desks when Agent Cutter entered their office.

"We have Patrick," he said.

12

The two partners were shocked. "How'd you find him? Are you sure it's him?" Vitrano asked.

"We're sure. We didn't find him. He was given to us. Do you know a man named Jack Stephano?"

They both whispered, "Yes."

"Do you work with him?"

They both shook their heads.

"You're lucky. Stephano's men found Patrick, tortured him, almost killed him, and then gave him to us."

"What about the money?" Bogan asked.

"We don't know anything about it. We'll watch Stephano. Maybe he'll lead us to the money."

Vitrano and Bogan stared at the table, thinking. Patrick had stolen ninety million dollars—too much money for one person to spend. There must be millions left.

"The money will be easy to find," Vitrano said. "Somebody was buried in Patrick's grave. Patrick killed him. It's clearly a death penalty case in Mississippi. Patrick will talk to avoid the death penalty."

Cutter looked at his watch. "I have to go," he said. "I have to give Trudy the good news."

When Patrick was killed in a car crash with no witnesses, his wife Trudy received 2.5 million dollars from his life insurance. She immediately bought an expensive house and an expensive car. She was excited about her good fortune.

Lance, Trudy's boyfriend, opened the door when Cutter knocked.

"Agent Cutter, FBI. I've come to see Trudy."

"She's in there," Lance said, pointing to the garage.

Cutter went to the garage, and Lance followed. "I'm Special Agent Cutter, FBI. I have some wonderful news for you," Cutter said with a broad smile. "We've found your husband, Mrs. Lanigan, and he's alive."

"You're lying," Lance said.

"No, I'm not. He's in Puerto Rico and should be back here in a week. I thought you should hear the good news before we tell the press."

Shocked and pale, Trudy sat down. Lance went to her, and Cutter left. It was obvious that she felt no joy at the news of Patrick's return. Only fear of losing the insurance money.

A few hours later, Trudy and Lance went to see her lawyer. "I want to file for divorce as fast as possible," she told him.

"That's not a problem," Riddleton said. "I'll do it in the morning." He knew that the divorce wasn't her biggest worry. "How much did you get in life insurance?" he asked.

"Why is that important?"

"Because they're going to sue you to get it back. He isn't dead, Trudy. If there's no death, there's no life insurance."

"They can't do that, can they?" she asked.

"Oh yes, they can, and they'll do it quickly. They'll take everything you've bought with the money as well as any money you still have."

Trudy's mouth fell open, and tears came to her eyes. "They just can't," she whispered.

♦

Before the press conference, Cutter and Maurice Mast, the US Attorney for the district, met with Raymond Sweeney, the local Sheriff, and T. L. Parrish, the local District Attorney, to decide what to do about Patrick.

"We have two big mysteries, two questions that must be answered," Parrish said. "The big one is money. Where is it? What did he do with it? Can we recover it and give it to its owners? The second mystery is who's buried in Patrick's grave? Only Patrick can tell us that, and he won't unless he's forced to. He must be scared, Maurice. Parchman's a frightening place. Patrick won't want to go to Parchman."

Everyone in the room knew about the horrors of the local prison. Patrick would realize that if he talked he might be sent to a government prison instead—one that wasn't so terrible. Parrish and Mast made a plan to work together. The FBI would continue its search for the money. The locals would concentrate on the murder.

Mast and Parrish went together to the press conference. Mast spoke first. "We're pleased to announce the capture of Mr. Patrick S. Lanigan, formerly of Biloxi. He's alive and well, and we have him in a hospital." He paused and then told them the details of Patrick's capture. He didn't mention that the FBI wasn't responsible for finding Patrick.

Parrish promised a quick indictment for murder.

Patrick's story was the big news that day. LANIGAN BACK FROM THE DEAD, the newspapers reported on the front page. There were stories about Patrick's capture and Trudy's request for a divorce. The law firm partners were suing Patrick for the return of their thirty million dollars; Northern Case Insurance was suing Trudy for the return of their money; Benny Aricia was suing Patrick for the return of his sixty million dollars; and Monarch-Sierra Insurance wanted to recover the four million dollars they paid the law firm when Patrick stole their money.

The story was also on all the TV stations. CNN played it nationally, and then internationally. Eva saw the report in her hotel room in Zurich. She was tired and scared; she wanted to go home but knew she couldn't. How much had he told them? How badly was he hurt? She whispered a prayer of thanks that Patrick was still alive.

♦

15

The next day Parrish, Sweeney, and Cutter met with a grand jury.* Parrish showed the members of the jury photos of the 1992 car crash. "We thought this burned body was Patrick," he told them, "but now we know we were wrong."

After a few questions, the jury voted to indict Patrick for capital murder—murder while committing another crime.

♦

Trudy was anxious and was taking drugs to help her stay calm. Reporters and photographers were around her house all the time. She didn't hate Patrick, but she didn't want him in her life again. And she didn't want to lose the insurance money. Her lawyer would have to find a way for her to keep the money.

Chapter 5   The Base Hospital

Patrick walked down the hospital hall with the help of Luis, his nurse. His skin was burned in four places, and his whole body ached. He stopped and looked out a window. Yes, he'd admitted that the money still existed. With electricity running through his body, he'd told them what happened to the money after he stole it. He couldn't remember the last part of his torture. He'd been near death. He'd called her name, but was it to himself or aloud? Where was she now?

When they returned to his room, Luis closed the door and curtains and took out a camera. Luis had agreed to take the photos when Patrick offered him five hundred dollars.

"Start there," Patrick told him, pointing to the bottom of the bed. "Get the whole body, including the face." Luis did as he was

---

* Grand jury: a jury that decides if there is enough evidence for a trial.

told and worked quickly. When he finished, he took the film to a photo shop.

◆

Sandy McDermott had read reports about the discovery of his law school friend with great interest. He was busy in his New Orleans office when his secretary announced that a woman from Brazil was waiting to see him.

"My name's Leah," she said quietly. "Patrick sent me."

Sandy noticed that she didn't smile and her eyes were tired. "Have you spoken to him since—"

"No. Not since he was taken. I want to hire you to be Patrick's lawyer."

"I'm available." Sandy had a lot of questions, but he knew he couldn't ask them now.

"You might be threatened by some very nasty people," she told him.

"Who?"

"The people chasing Patrick."

"I think they've caught him," he said.

"Yes, but they don't have the money."

"I understand," he said. So, the money hadn't been spent; that wasn't surprising. But how much was left? "Where is the money?" he asked.

"You can't ask that question," she said.

"What do you want me to do for him?"

"Everything. Patrick wants no other lawyer."

"Then I'm hired. We're old friends, you know."

"Good. We can't meet here again. There are people trying to find me because they think I can lead them to the money. So we'll meet in other places." Leah looked at her watch. "There's a flight to Miami in three hours. We can talk on the plane."

"Where are we going?"

17

"You'll go to San Juan to see Patrick. I'll go another direction."

On the plane Sandy and Leah didn't talk much. Just before landing in Miami, she said, "I won't see you again for a few days. I have to keep moving. Patrick will give you instructions, and he and I will communicate through you. Be careful. When people learn that you're his lawyer, you'll attract the attention of the people who are looking for me."

"Who are they?" he asked.

"Patrick will tell you."

"You have the money, don't you?"

"I can't answer that question."

When they landed, she shook his hand and said, "Tell Patrick I'm fine." Then she disappeared into the crowd.

◆

When he landed in San Juan, Sandy went to the Navy base to visit Patrick. The two old friends hadn't seen each other for six years. Patrick sat in his bed in the dark room. He kept a sheet over his body. Sandy studied his face. It was thin, and the chin and nose were different. He looked like someone else. But his eyes and voice were the same.

"Thanks for coming," Patrick said.

"Sure," Sandy replied. "She said to tell you she's fine," he added. Patrick closed his eyes and said a prayer of thanks. Then he was silent. Sandy sat and waited for his friend. He was alive, and right now nothing else mattered.

After a time, Sandy wanted to talk. "A lot of people are waiting for you back in Biloxi," he said. "Trudy filed for divorce two days ago. The grand jury has indicted you for capital murder."

"I know," said Patrick. "CNN has kept me informed."

Sandy paused and then asked, "When do you want to talk?"

18

Patrick rolled to his side and looked at the wall. "They tortured me, Sandy," he said quietly. "They taped wires to my body and gave me electric shocks until I talked. Here, look." He lifted his left arm so Sandy could inspect the burn marks. "They kept asking about the money. I'm afraid I told them about the girl, Sandy."

"The lawyer? Leah?"

"Yes, I'm almost certain I told them about Leah."

"Told who, Patrick?" Sandy asked.

Patrick closed his eyes as pain returned to his legs. He gently rolled over onto his back again and pulled the sheet down to his waist. "Look, Sandy," he said, pointing to two bad burns on his chest. "Here's the proof."

Sandy turned on a table lamp, leaned closer, and looked. "Who did this?" he asked again.

"I don't know. A bunch of people." Patrick felt sorry for his friend. Sandy wanted to know what had happened—about the torture and about what had happened four years ago. It was a wonderful story, but he wasn't sure how much he could tell. No one knew the details of the car crash. But he could tell his lawyer about his capture and torture. He said, "Sit closer and turn off that lamp. The light bothers me." Then he told the story of his kidnapping.

At six o'clock the next morning, Patrick's doctor entered his room. He checked his wounds and said, "You're ready to go. They have good doctors waiting for you where you're going." Then he left.

Thirty minutes later, Agent Brent Myers from the Biloxi office walked in. "Good morning, Patrick. I just talked to your doctor. You're going home tomorrow, and I've got orders to take you back. We'll leave in the morning on a special Air Force plane to Biloxi. See you early in the morning." Myers left.

Next, Luis arrived with coffee and fruit. He put a package under Patrick's sheet and asked if he needed anything else.

"No," Patrick said, thanking him softly.

An hour later, Sandy arrived.

"I want you to go home immediately," Patrick said. "And take this with you." He handed Sandy the package.

Sandy sat down, opened it, and looked through the photos. "Who did this to you?" he asked.

"Whose prisoner am I?"

"The FBI's."

"So, I think the FBI did it to me. My own government found me, caught me, tortured me, and is now taking me back. Look at what they've done to me."

"You should sue them for this," Sandy said.

"For millions. And quickly. Here's the plan: I'm leaving for Biloxi in the morning. We should file our lawsuit late this afternoon so it'll be in the paper tomorrow. Tell the press. I've marked two photos. Give them to the reporters for the Coast paper—the one that's read by the people who will be on my jury. People will feel sorry for me—an American citizen tortured by the FBI."

Sandy studied Patrick's face. "It wasn't really the FBI, was it?" he asked.

"No," Patrick said, "it wasn't. I was delivered to the FBI by some people whose names I don't know. They'd been chasing me for a long time. And they're still waiting out there somewhere."

"Does the FBI know about them?"

"Yes," Patrick said. He paused. "Be careful. I've hidden a lot of money, Sandy. There are people who'll do anything to find it."

"How much of the money is left?" Sandy asked.

"All of it. And more."

"We may need it to save you," Sandy said.

"I have a plan."

"I'm sure you do. See you in Biloxi."

Chapter 6   Return to Biloxi

Newspaper, TV, and radio reporters waited in the courthouse while Sandy filed the lawsuit. They listened carefully as he calmly informed them that his client was suing the FBI for physical damage and torture. Sandy answered questions and then reached into his case and removed two large color photos.

"This is what they did to Patrick," he said. The cameras moved closer. "This is your government—FBI agents—at work, ladies and gentlemen, torturing an American citizen."

Everyone was shocked. Almost half of the six o'clock news was about Sandy and the photos. The other half was about Patrick's return the next day. CNN played the story hourly.

Hamilton Jaynes was at his club when he saw the news. He wasn't happy. The FBI sued by Patrick Lanigan? He excused himself and went to his office. He made a phone call, and two agents went immediately to Jack Stephano's front door.

Stephano had watched the reports and wasn't surprised to see the FBI. He thought it was funny that the FBI was being blamed for his men's work. He also thought it was a good idea of Patrick's. "Good evening," he said politely.

"FBI," the first man said. "Mr. Jaynes would like to see you."

"Why?"

"We don't know," the second man said. "He told us to find you and take you to his office. Can you come with us?"

Stephano was angry, but he reminded himself that there were already criminal charges against him because of the Lanigan case. A little more cooperation might help. "Give me five minutes," he said.

When Stephano entered his office, Jaynes dropped the thick report he was looking at. It was almost midnight. "What did you do to that boy down there?"

"I don't know. I guess the Brazilian boys got a little rough. He'll live."

"This is serious business, OK, Jack? These allegations are terrible. Right now, the whole country is looking at those pictures and wondering why we tortured an American citizen. Who did it?"

"Some local people down there. I don't know their names," Stephano said without concern. He could bargain his way out of any trouble from the FBI. He had very good lawyers.

"The Director has suggested we make an agreement," Jaynes said. "We're prepared to arrest Benny Aricia tomorrow. We'll tell the press how this guy, who lost ninety million dollars, hired you to find Lanigan. And when you caught him, you tried to make him talk but still didn't find the money."

Stephano listened without expression.

"Then we'll arrest the CEOs★ of Monarch-Sierra Insurance and Northern Case Insurance. Those are the two other members of your group, we understand. We'll tell the press that these guys helped Aricia finance your man's trip to Brazil to get Patrick. Think of it, Stephano, your clients will all be arrested. You'll be out of business."

"So what do you want?" Stephano asked, wondering how Jaynes knew so much about his clients.

"Here's the plan. You tell us everything—how you found Patrick, how much he told you—everything. And we'll drop the charges against you and leave your clients alone."

There were lots of reasons to accept this plan. One was that Mrs. Stephano was crazier than before about the FBI men watching their house. "I'll have to talk to my attorney," Stephano said.

"You have until 5 P.M. tomorrow."

◆

Patrick's story was in most of the newspapers in the Western

★CEO: the CEO of a company is its highest ranking officer.

world. Eva read the news in an American paper while drinking coffee at a café in Aix, France. The story described the burns but didn't print the photos. Her heart broke, and she put on dark glasses to hide her eyes.

Patrick was going home. And she would go, too. She'd stay in the background, hiding, doing what he wanted and praying for the safety of both of them.

◆

The doctor gave Patrick pills to make him comfortable for the flight and a file with his medical records. Patrick thanked him. He shook hands with Luis and said good-bye.

Agent Myers was waiting outside the door with four Navy policemen. "If you behave, I won't put chains on you now," he said. "When we land, though, I have no choice."

"Thanks," Patrick said. His legs ached and his knees were weak, but he held his head high and his back straight as he walked down the hall and out to the waiting van.

As the van drove slowly across the base, Patrick thought about his life in Ponta Pora, his home now. He wondered what jail they'd put him in in Biloxi. Then he had an idea. He opened the file and quickly read the doctor's notes. *Patient should remain hospitalized for at least another week*, the doctor had written. This would keep him out of jail. He had to tell Sandy to arrange a comfortable, private room for him.

"I need to make a phone call," he said.

When the van stopped, he and Myers went to a small office and faxed the doctor's instructions to Sandy. Then they climbed the steps into the Air Force plane.

The plane landed at Keesler Air Force base outside Biloxi. Patrick was surprised there wasn't a crowd waiting for him. He wanted the press to see him with chains on his legs and wrists. But they'd been forbidden to come near the plane. Only Agent Cutter,

Sheriff Sweeney, two Air Force officers, and Sandy were there.

"Hello, Patrick. Welcome home," the Sheriff said.

"Hello, Raymond," Patrick answered with a smile. They knew each other well.

Cutter started to introduce himself, but as soon as Patrick heard "FBI" he turned to Sandy. They all got into the waiting van.

Patrick was glad the chase was over. Lots of problems were ahead, but, for now, he could ignore what was behind him. Patrick had never been able to completely relax and enjoy his new life. Not even the money could calm his fears. He'd always known that this day would come. He'd stolen too much money. He looked out the window as he rode along, and he suddenly missed Rua Tiradentes.

Sandy reached into his case and removed the Coast paper. LANIGAN SUES FBI FOR TORTURE was at the top of the front page, which was full of Patrick's story and the photos. Patrick admired it.

The van stopped at the entrance to the base hospital, and Patrick was taken to his room. Guards were at the door. Sandy stayed with Patrick.

"I'd like to see my mother," Patrick said.

"She's on her way. What about your wife and daughter?"

"I'd like to see Ashley Nicole, but not now. She was only two when I left. I'm sure she doesn't remember me. For obvious reasons, I'd rather not see Trudy."

There was a knock on the door, and Sheriff Sweeney entered, holding a thick pile of papers.

"Sorry to bother you, but I need to give you these. First, this is an indictment from the grand jury for capital murder." He handed it to Patrick, and continued. "This is a lawsuit for divorce, filed by Trudy Lanigan."

"What a surprise," Patrick said, as he took it. Without looking at the papers, he passed them to Sandy.

24

"These are lawsuits filed by Mr. Benjamin Aricia, your old law firm, and Monarch-Sierra Insurance. Sorry, Patrick."

Patrick took them and passed them to Sandy. "Is that all?"

"For now." They shook hands, and the Sheriff left.

Sandy looked through the papers. "It seems that Trudy's really upset with you. She wants you out of her life."

"I've tried my best. What reasons does she give?"

"You left her. Mental cruelty. Are you planning to fight it?"

"That depends on what she wants."

Sandy turned another page. "Well, she wants you to give up your parental rights. She wants all property you owned together at the time of your disappearance and a reasonable percent of anything you've got since then. That's all."

"I'll give her the divorce, Sandy, and gladly. But it won't be as easy as she thinks."

"What are you planning?"

"We'll talk about it later. I'm tired. I need to rest now. Mom will be here in a minute."

"When do you think we can meet again?" Sandy asked.

"How about tomorrow morning?"

Sandy put the papers in his case. "I'll be here at ten."

Half an hour later Patrick's mother arrived, and they had a tearful meeting. He asked about aunts and uncles, people he hadn't thought about in the past four years. They were anxious to see him. Patrick thought that was odd because they'd never been anxious to see him before.

Chapter 7   Patrick's First Appearance

Cutter and Ted Grimshaw, chief investigator for the district, carefully examined the evidence from Patrick's death. There wasn't much. No one suspected murder when Patrick died, so there was no effort to gather physical clues. There were ten large color photos of the burned-out Chevy Blazer. After the car burned, there was very little left of the body in it, and that was buried. So now they had no idea who'd died in the crash.

Patrick had spent that weekend in an old cabin near the edge of the forest outside Biloxi. Sunday night, February 9, 1992, he called to tell his wife he was leaving the cabin. He stopped at Verhall's Country Store and bought fifty liters of gasoline. An hour later, Patrick's Chevy Blazer was found burning at the bottom of a steep hill twelve kilometers down the road. The fire was so hot that they couldn't rescue the driver. They read the license plate, and at 3:30 A.M. Trudy received the call that made her a widow.

The next day, they discovered a shoe near the Blazer. When they showed it to Trudy, she recognized it as Patrick's and cried. His funeral was the following day.

◆

Dr. Hayani was happy to sit and chat with Patrick. He enjoyed being close to this patient who was in all the news reports. He encouraged Patrick to talk about his experience.

"The torture was something I could never accurately describe," Patrick said after an hour. "Sleep is impossible. I hear voices, then I smell my flesh burning, and then I wake up. And it's not getting any better. They're still out there, still after me. I can't sleep. I don't want to sleep. I'll get tortured again." He paused. "Doc, I need to stay here as long as I can. They'll want to put me in jail—in a cell with other criminals. I can't live like that."

"But why do they want to move you?"

"It's pressure, Doc. They have to slowly increase the pressure on me until I tell them what they want. If they put me in a cell with criminals, I'll understand that I have to talk to them. If I don't, I'll spend the rest of my life at Parchman, the worst place in

26

the world. But you can keep me here, Doc. Just tell the Judge I need to remain in your care, and I can stay here. Please, Doc."

Hayani couldn't believe that this kind man could kill someone. "Of course, Patrick," he said.

◆

The boy's mother was Neldene Crouch. She said her son had been missing since Sunday, February 9, 1992, the same day Patrick Lanigan died. His name was Pepper Scarboro. He was seventeen when he disappeared.

There was no good evidence that Pepper and Patrick had ever met. However, Pepper's gun, tent, and sleeping bag were found in Patrick's cabin in late February of 1992. The two disappeared at about the same time, from the same area. Cutter and Sweeney were almost positive that Pepper had died in Patrick's car, but they couldn't prove it.

Neldene, however, thought she could, and was anxious to share her ideas with the press. Her lawyer held a press conference. Neldene cried, and her lawyer suggested there might be legal action against Patrick Lanigan. He had obviously killed Pepper and burned his body to hide the evidence so he could steal ninety million dollars.

The press loved it. They were given pictures of young Pepper. Now there was a face for the dead body, and he became human. This was the boy Patrick had killed.

Patrick watched the story alone in his dark room. He and Pepper had met several times, beginning in January of 1992. They'd hunted together and talked. He wasn't surprised that people believed he'd killed the kid.

◆

For the third day, Patrick didn't wash his hair or shave. The world was waiting to see him today. He wore the same clothes he'd worn every day. He didn't wear socks; he wanted people to see the rope marks just above his ankles.

Sandy arrived at ten and gave Patrick a pair of dark glasses he'd requested. Patrick sat on the edge of his bed and tried to breathe slowly. "I never thought this day would come. Never," he said.

"I'll do all the talking," Sandy said. "Just try and relax."

Sheriff Sweeney knocked and entered with his assistants. Patrick put on the dark glasses and was led out of the building to a waiting car. Sandy stayed on his left, gently holding him by the elbow.

Patrick looked out the window as they drove through Biloxi, and noticed the changes since he'd left. He started to relax. Then they turned onto Main Street, and he was anxious again. In the middle of the old shops and stores was the large white building where he'd been a partner in Bogan, Rapley, Vitrano, Havarac, and Lanigan, Attorneys.

The car stopped in front of the courthouse, where a crowd of reporters, photographers, and cameramen was waiting. Patrick lowered his head and tried to hide among the Sheriff's assistants. They walked him quickly into the courthouse as the press called out questions: "Patrick, what's it like to be home?" "Where's the money?" "Who burned in the car?"

Sandy and Sheriff Sweeney stayed with Patrick in the jury room. "Are you OK, Patrick?" Sweeney asked.

"Yes, sure, Raymond, thanks." He sounded scared, and his hands and knees shook.

There was a knock on the door, and a pretty girl entered and said, "Welcome back, Patrick. Judge Huskey would like to meet with you. He'll be here in a few minutes."

She and Sweeney left and closed the door. Finally Patrick was alone with his lawyer. "A couple of things. First, Leah will contact you soon. I've written her a long letter, and I'd like you to give it to her."

"OK."

"Second, there's a small machine for finding bugs, called a DX-130. It costs about six hundred dollars. Get one, and bring it with you whenever we meet. We'll get rid of bugs in the room and phones before each conference. Also, hire someone to check your office twice a week. It's very expensive, but I'll pay for it. Any questions?"

"No."

There was another knock, and Judge Karl Huskey entered. Patrick smiled. He was desperate to see his old friend.

"Good to see you, Patrick," Huskey said warmly as they shook hands. "How are you?"

"I've had better days, but it's good to see you. Even in these circumstances."

Huskey was glad to know that his friend wasn't dead. He was worried about the capital murder charge. They could deal with the divorce and other lawsuits, but not murder.

"Do you plan to enter a plea of not guilty?" he asked.

"Yes, I do."

"Then it will be a routine first appearance and will take less than ten minutes."

Judge Huskey was often sympathetic toward ordinary people who'd committed awful crimes. He wanted to help, to forgive. But this was Patrick, his old friend. He almost had tears in his eyes. He kneeled next to him and said, "Patrick, I can't be the judge for this case, for obvious reasons. Right now, I'll handle the matters before the trial to make sure you're protected. I'm still your friend. Don't hesitate to call."

"Thanks, Karl," Patrick said, biting his lip. Karl stood and headed for the door. "Are there a lot of people out there?"

"Yes, Patrick. Friends and enemies. They're all out there."

◆

Crowded courtrooms were not uncommon for trials, but no one could remember such a crowded room for a simple first appearance. The press had taken the best seats. Many lawyers were there just to see Patrick. The papers had been full of stories about him for four days. The torture story had increased their curiosity.

Charles Bogan and Doug Vitrano sat together. They'd wanted to sit in the front row to make eye contact with Patrick and threaten him quietly, but they were in the fifth. A few other lawyers had come to give Patrick their support. Escape was a common dream of many small-town lawyers. At least Patrick had had the courage to chase the dream.

Many other people were present who'd hardly known Patrick but now suddenly claimed to have been his friends.

The door opened, and Sheriff Sweeney entered, holding Patrick by the elbow. Sandy followed. Patrick walked slowly, head down, across the room to the defendant's table. He sat down, his shoulders low, chin down. Sandy put his arm on his shoulder.

The door opened again, and T. L. Parrish, the District Attorney, entered alone. He walked to his table next to Patrick's and sat beside Sheriff Sweeney. Behind him were agents Joshua Cutter, Brent Myers, and two others.

Judge Huskey entered and sat down. "State against Patrick S. Lanigan. Would the defendant please rise?" Patrick slowly stood. "Mr. Lanigan, I'm holding a copy of an indictment against you by the grand jury. It states that you murdered a human being, name unknown. Have you read this indictment and discussed it with your attorney?"

"Yes, sir," Patrick announced.

"What is your plea?"

"Not guilty."

"Your plea of not guilty is accepted. You may sit down." He paused. "Any questions from the attorneys?"

The lawyers said nothing. Parrish stood and said, "Your

Honor,* we would like to put the accused in jail as soon as possible. As you know, he's at the base hospital now—"

"I just talked to his doctor, Mr. Parrish. He's receiving medical treatment. As soon as his doctor gives permission, we'll move him to the jail."

"Thank you, Judge."

"If there's nothing else, this hearing is closed."

◆

When they offered her 50,000 dollars, Trudy agreed to talk to a TV journalist. The show was *Inside Stories*, which was very popular. Her daughter, Ashley Nicole, sat on the sofa with Trudy. "Look real sad now," journalist Nancy De Angelo told the little girl. "We need tears from you," she told Trudy.

They chatted for an hour about all the terrible things Patrick was doing to them. Trudy cried when she talked about the funeral. She had suffered through the months and years afterward. No, she hadn't remarried. No, she hadn't heard from her husband since he'd returned. She wasn't sure if she wanted to. No, he'd made no effort to see his daughter. And she cried again. She hated the thought of divorce, but what could she do? And the lawsuit, how terrible! This nasty insurance company really wanted to destroy her. Patrick was such a terrible person. If they found the money, did she expect to get any of it? Of course not! She was shocked by the suggestion.

On TV, the interview was twenty minutes. Patrick watched it in his dark hospital room. It made him smile.

◆

Sandy's secretary was cutting out his photo and the story of

---

*Your Honor: a title used when talking to a judge.

yesterday's court appearance from the New Orleans paper when the phone call came. She found him immediately.

It was Leah Pires. She said hello and asked if he'd had his office checked for bugs. Sandy said yes. She was in a hotel room a few blocks away and suggested that they meet there. Sandy was excited to hear her voice and would do whatever she wanted.

Leah greeted him with a smile and poured coffee for both of them. "How is he?" she asked.

"He's getting better. The doctor says he'll be fine."

"How bad was it?" she asked quietly.

"Pretty bad." He reached into his case, removed a file, and handed it to her. She looked at the photos and cried.

"Poor Patrick," she said to herself. "Poor baby."

"I'm sorry," Sandy said. "Here's a letter from Patrick."

She finished crying and poured more coffee. "Are any of the injuries permanent?" she asked.

"The doctor thinks they'll get better with time."

"Mentally, how is he?"

"He's OK. He doesn't sleep much and has bad dreams. But he's getting better. I guess he's lucky to be alive."

"He always said they wouldn't kill him." She paused and changed the subject. "Let's talk about his divorce." She stood, walked to a drawer, removed a thick file, and placed it in front of Sandy. "Did you see Trudy on TV?" she asked.

"Yes."

"Patrick hates her. She's a bad person, and she was unfaithful to him the whole time they were married. It's all in this file. The last year they were together, Patrick hired an investigator to watch her. There are photographs of her lover, Lance Maxa, coming and going from Patrick's house when he was away. There are also pictures of Lance and Trudy sitting by Patrick's pool—without clothes."

Sandy took the file and looked through it until he found the photographs. He smiled. "This will help."

"Patrick wants the divorce, you understand. He won't fight it. But she needs to be silenced."

"This should keep her quiet. What about the child?"

"Patrick loves Ashley Nicole, but there's one problem. He's not the father."

"Who is?"

"Probably Lance. He and Trudy have been together for a long time. Even in high school."

"How does he know he's not the father?"

"When the child was fourteen months old, Patrick obtained a drop of her blood. He sent it, with a drop of his, to a laboratory for DNA★ tests. He's definitely not the father of the child. The report's in the file."

Sandy had to walk around and think. He stood at the window and watched the traffic. "If he doesn't want the child, why are you mentioning this?"

"You talk about this only to her lawyer," she said. "You show him the file, all of it. Then they'll be anxious to come to a settlement."

"What type of settlement?"

"She gets nothing."

"What could she get?"

"It depends. It could be a small fortune, or a large one."

"It would be helpful if you guys would tell me more."

"We will. I promise. But first, we'll take care of the divorce. Trudy has to give up any claim to anything of Patrick's. Get that done, and we'll chat again next week."

It was suddenly time for Sandy to leave. "How long will you be here?" he asked.

"Not long," she said and handed him an envelope. "That's a

★ DNA: DNA carries information in cells about a living thing.

33

letter for Patrick. Tell him I'm fine, I'm moving around, and I haven't seen anyone following me."

Sandy took the envelope. Leah was nervous and was anxious for him to leave. She forced a smile and said, "You have a job to do. Patrick and I will worry about the rest."

Chapter 8   Stephano's Story

Stephano's lawyer advised him to accept the FBI's arrangement. The criminal charges against him would be dropped, and there would be no charges against his clients. He would tell the FBI everything he knew about the search for and capture of Patrick Lanigan.

Stephano had easily persuaded Benny Aricia that the FBI was going to arrest him soon. It was more difficult to persuade Paul Atterson at Monarch-Sierra Insurance and Frank Jill at Northern Case Insurance. Jaynes sent agents to both offices to ask questions about the search for and capture of Patrick Lanigan. Both called Stephano by noon and told him to fully cooperate with the FBI.

For four years Stephano had worked with these men. He'd earned almost a million dollars, he'd spent another 2.5 million of his clients' money, and he could claim success. They'd found Lanigan. They hadn't found the ninety million, but it hadn't been spent. There was a chance of recovering it.

♦

Benny Aricia came to see Stephano in his office. He'd listened to the torture tape three times. He was certain Patrick had told what he knew, and it wasn't enough. Patrick knew he'd someday be caught; that's why he'd placed the money with the girl, who hid it from everyone—including Patrick. It was a great plan.

"How much will it take to find her?" he asked Stephano.

"I'd guess a hundred thousand, with no guarantees. We have no idea where she is, but we know where she's from. And we know she'll probably go to Biloxi."

"Will the FBI know we're still looking?"

"No."

"And if you find her?"

"We'll make her talk," Stephano said, and they smiled.

Stephano honestly planned to tell most of what he knew. He knew little—just the name of the Brazilian lawyer who had the money. Now she'd disappeared, and he doubted the FBI would follow her. The money didn't belong to them. And he wanted the FBI out of his life. Mrs. Stephano was extremely anxious. If he didn't reopen his office quickly, he'd be out of business. So, he planned to tell them what they wanted to hear, most of it anyway. He'd take Benny's money and chase the girl. Maybe he'd get lucky. And he'd send some men to New Orleans to watch Lanigan's lawyer. The FBI didn't need to know these little details.

◆

Stephano sat at a table in the FBI office, his lawyer beside him.

"What does your company do?" asked Underhill.

"Lots of things," Stephano said. "Watch people. Get information. Find missing persons."

"Were you hired to find Patrick Lanigan?"

"Yes. On March 28, 1992."

"Who hired you?"

"Benny Aricia, the man whose money was stolen."

"What did you do after you were hired?"

"I immediately flew to Nassau in the Bahamas to meet with the manager of the bank where the theft took place."

"Why did Aricia have an account outside the US?"

"It was ninety million dollars. Nobody wanted the money to appear in a bank in Biloxi."

"Where did it come from?"

"Here, in Washington. The wire began at nine-thirty on the morning of March 26, 1992. At fifteen minutes after ten, it reached the United Bank, where it sat for nine minutes before it was wired to a bank in Malta. From there, it was wired to Panama."

"How did the money get wired out of the bank?"

"Someone, Mr. Lanigan we think, prepared false wiring instructions from my client's lawyers, his old firm, and rerouted the money. On the morning the money was wired, he presented himself as Doug Vitrano, one of his partners. He had a perfect passport and driver's license, and he knew all about the money which was being wired from Washington. He had a paper from the office giving him permission to accept the money for the firm and then wire it to the bank in Malta. The other partners, of course, thought he was dead. They had no reason to suspect anyone was after the money. The settlement which produced the ninety million was extremely secret, and only a few people knew exactly when or where the money was wired."

"So you went to Biloxi to look for clues, and you found that the law offices were bugged."

"We did. We had two jobs: first, to find Mr. Lanigan and the money, and second, to find out how he'd stolen it. There were twenty-two bugs in the offices—in every phone, in every office, under every desk."

"Did you find out where the signals went?" he asked.

"No. But I think he rented a boat. He needed a place to hide and listen to the conversations. A boat is simple and safe. The office is only 600 meters from the beach, and there are a lot of boats out there."

"Do you have any evidence he used a boat?"

"We found a small company in Alabama that rented a sailboat to a man on February 11, 1992, the day Lanigan was buried. We showed the manager a picture. He said maybe it was Patrick, but he couldn't be positive. The beard was gone, the hair was dark, and he wore glasses and was overweight."

"What happened to the boat?"

"A kid working at the dock said the man brought the boat back on either March 24 or 25 and was never seen again."

"Where did Patrick go?"

"He left the area. He took the name of Doug Vitrano. On the twenty-fifth he flew to Nassau, using tickets in Vitrano's name. He was at the bank when it opened at nine o'clock. He moved the money and took a flight to New York at 2:30 P.M. Then he stopped using Vitrano's name and used another. We lost him."

◆

While Stephano talked in Washington, Benny Aricia and Guy settled in rooms in Biloxi. They believed the girl would have to come there. Patrick wasn't going anywhere. She'd have to come to him. And they had to catch her when she did.

Osmar and his boys were still in Rio, watching the same places each day. If she came back, they'd see her.

◆

Benny Aricia had moved to the Coast in 1985 as an officer of Platt & Rockwell, a big defense contractor with a history of overbilling and false claims. One of their small divisions had received a 990 million dollar Navy contract, and Benny was responsible for it. He hated contracting with the government, and he hated living in Biloxi. In 1988 he asked for a different job and was denied. He studied the False Claims Act. This encouraged people to report overbilling in government contracts. Then he went to Charles Bogan for help filing a claim with the government.

The lawsuit was filed in September of 1990 with the

37

allegation that 600 million dollars had been overbilled. If Benny could prove this, he'd receive 15 percent of that amount, and one-third of that would go to the law firm. Bogan gave information to the press, and the company lost business. After a year, Platt & Rockwell agreed to repay the 600 million dollars. Benny got ready to receive his fortune, and Bogan and the partners got ready to spend theirs. Then Patrick disappeared, and so did their money.

♦

Stephano's next questioner was Warren. "When did your group form?" he asked.

"After we lost Patrick in New York, we waited. Nothing happened. I'd met with Benny Aricia, and he'd agreed to pay a million dollars to finance the search. Then I met with people from Monarch-Sierra and Northern Case. Northern Case had already paid 2.5 million to the widow. They couldn't sue to get it back because there wasn't strong evidence he was still alive. They agreed to give us half a million. Monarch-Sierra carried the law firm's insurance, protecting them from theft by its employees and partners. They had to pay four million dollars to the firm and agreed to pay another million to finance the search."

"How was the money spent?"

"On salaries, travel, rewards, and the services of my firm. Not much is left."

"Tell me about the rewards."

"We immediately offered a 100,000 dollar reward for any information about the disappearance of Patrick Lanigan. We heard nothing for months, and then in August of '92 Bogan got a call from a lawyer whose client knew something. His client was a young woman who worked in a book store. Sometime in January of '92 she noticed a customer in the travel and language section. When another customer entered the store, he tried to hide

38

behind a shelf, but the other man saw him. 'Patrick, it's been a long time,' he said, and the two men talked about their law careers.

"The one called Patrick was anxious and left as soon as he could. Three nights later, he came back, picked out a language course, paid for it, and left quickly. Three weeks after that, the girl saw in the paper that Patrick Lanigan had been killed in a terrible car crash, and she recognized his picture. Then, six weeks later, there was a story about the stolen money. When she learned about the reward, she went to her lawyer."

"So what was the language?"

"Brazilian Portuguese."

Chapter 9   The Divorce

Sweeney and Grimshaw visited Patrick. They photographed him and took his fingerprints. Then the two men joined Cutter in his office, where an FBI fingerprint man was waiting for them. When Pepper's gun was found in Patrick's cabin, Grimshaw had taken fingerprints from it. The fingerprint man compared those with Patrick's.

"Several of these are perfect matches," he said. "The gun was covered with Lanigan's prints."

Certainly good news, they thought.

♦

Patrick demanded a different room for all future meetings with his attorney, and Dr. Hayani quickly made the necessary arrangements. Patrick also requested a wheelchair. A nurse pushed him to the room where Sandy was waiting.

"Did you get the machine for finding bugs?" Patrick asked.

"It'll be here in a few days. You should relax a little. You've lived in fear, always looking over your shoulder. But those days are over. They caught you. Relax."

"They're still out there. They have me, but not the money. And the money's much more important. They won't rest until they have it. The people who lost their money have spent a fortune trying to find it."

"How do you know? Who are they?"

There was a long pause. "Sit down," Patrick said.

Sandy removed the thick file Leah had given him four hours earlier, and Patrick recognized it immediately. "When did you see her?" he asked anxiously.

"This morning. She's fine, sends her love, and says nobody's following her yet. She asked me to deliver this."

Patrick opened the envelope, pulled out a three-page letter, and read it. Sandy looked through the file and took out pictures of Trudy and Lance.

When Patrick finished reading, he said, "I have another letter for her." Then he saw the photos on the table. "Good work, isn't it?"

"It's amazing. I've never seen so much proof in a divorce case."

"Well, I learned about Lance after we'd been married almost two years. Trudy was going to have a baby, so I said nothing. But a year later, I started gathering evidence. I wasn't sure when I'd need it, but I knew the marriage was over. I left town every chance I could. She never seemed to mind."

"I'm meeting with her lawyer at 5 P.M."

"Good. Threaten everything, but get a settlement. She has to give up all rights, Sandy. She gets nothing of mine."

◆

Trudy's lawyer, J. Murray Riddleton, politely welcomed Sandy. "So how's Patrick? Have you found the money yet?" he asked, with a broad smile.

"Didn't know I was looking for any," Sandy said, and Riddleton laughed. "I saw your client on TV last night," Sandy continued. "We have no problems with her desire to get a divorce, and she can have the child. In fact, my client has no plans to visit the child."

"Smart man. After leaving her four years ago."

"There's another reason," Sandy said, as he opened the file and picked out the DNA test. He handed a copy to Riddleton, who'd stopped smiling. "Read this."

Riddleton read the report slowly and then looked up with an empty expression. "I'm sure this can be explained."

"I'm sure it cannot. Under Alabama law, the DNA test is enough evidence. If this is printed in the papers, it could be embarrassing for your client." He paused. "She can have the divorce. The kid, too."

"Oh, I understand. You're threatening us. If she stops demanding his money and property, he won't give this information to the press. He's crazy, and so are you."

Sandy looked through the file and took out another report and two large photos of Lance and Trudy without clothes. "These were taken by the pool at my client's home while he was in Dallas. Do you recognize these people?" Riddleton was silent. "There are more," Sandy promised. "And I have three other reports from private detectives. Your client would surely be embarrassed if these were on the news."

Riddleton breathed heavily. He knew he was defeated. "What does he want?"

"He wants her to stop talking, to get her divorce and go away, and to drop all future claims against him."

"Let me speak to her." Riddleton smiled sadly.

Sandy left, and Riddleton went to see Trudy and Lance. He told them Patrick knew she'd had a lover. Trudy acted shocked.

"Do you deny it?" Riddleton asked.

41

"Absolutely," she said.

"Of course," added Lance. "The man's lying."

"Patrick hired investigators," Riddleton told them, handing them one of the reports. Trudy and Lance looked at each other. They'd been caught, but they weren't ashamed.

"Can these investigators talk in court?" Lance asked.

"We're not going to court," Riddleton said.

"Why not?" Trudy asked.

"Because of these." Riddleton put the photos in front of them. They were shocked. Trudy started to cry. "He's not getting my daughter," she said.

"Relax," Riddleton said. "He doesn't want the kid. He's not the father."

They both thought about that while Riddleton got out a report. "He had a DNA test done." He looked at Lance and added, "Congratulations."

Trudy was angry. "So what do we do?"

"It's simple. You give up your right to his money and property, and he gives you the divorce and the kid."

"But I'm going to lose everything," she said. "Look what he's done to me. I got two and a half million when he died, and now the insurance company wants to take it all back. Can I sue him for mental cruelty?"

"No. Look, it's very simple. You get the divorce and the kid, and Patrick keeps whatever money is out there. And everything is private. If you don't agree, he'll give the reports and photos to the press."

"Where do I sign?" she asked.

♦

It was past time to leave for the day, but Dr. Hayani stopped to see his famous patient.

"Welcome to my office," Patrick said. He was sitting at a small table, which was now his desk. A pile of legal papers was in one corner.

"Nice," Hayani said. "How are you doing?"

"I'm fine," he answered, as he always did. Patrick sat on the edge of his bed and looked at his doctor. "Can I tell you something?" he asked sincerely.

"Certainly."

"When I was a lawyer," Patrick began softly, "I had a client who got caught stealing money from his bank. He was arrested at home, late at night, taken to jail, and put with some rough guys. They beat him. You can't let that happen to me, Doc." His eyes watered.

"Don't worry, Patrick, I won't. I promise."

Chapter 10   Patrick's Story

As Judge Karl Huskey drove to the hospital the next afternoon, he thought about how Patrick had changed physically in the months before his disappearance. He'd gained weight steadily. A month before he disappeared, he told Karl that he weighed 150 kilos. He grew a beard and let his hair grow long. He didn't look like the Patrick they found in Brazil.

Although others had forgotten about Patrick a few months after his disappearance, Karl had thought about his friend every day. It was hard to believe he was really back.

When he entered the dark room, Patrick was sitting in bed with his shirt off. "Thanks for coming," he said.

"Nasty burns," Karl said, as Patrick put his shirt on.

"It was ugly," Patrick said. "Doc says they're getting better. But I need to stay here."

"I have no problem with that, and I'm the one who decides where you stay."

Patrick seemed to relax a bit. "Thanks, Karl. You know I can't live in the jail. And I'll kill myself before I go to Parchman."

"I don't blame you. Let's talk about something pleasant."

"You said you can't keep this case. When will you give it to someone else? Who?"

"Soon. Probably Trussel." Karl stared at Patrick, who was unable to keep eye contact. This wasn't the same Patrick he'd known before. He decided to ask Patrick about his experiences. "Where'd you get that chin and nose?"

"Bought them in Rio. Do you like them?"

"They're handsome. I hear there are beautiful beaches in Brazil."

"Yes."

There was a long silence. Karl realized that Patrick was in no hurry to talk, but he couldn't sit silently in the dark room much longer. "Look, Patrick, I'm not here as your Judge. I'm not your lawyer. I'm your friend. You can talk to me."

"I guess it sounds romantic, doesn't it? Disappearing and becoming somebody new. All your problems are left behind. You dream about that, don't you, Karl?"

"I guess everybody does at some time. How long did you plan it?"

"A long time. I seriously doubted that the baby was mine." Karl looked surprised. "That's right. I'm not the father," Patrick continued. "I loved the child, but I knew Trudy wasn't faithful. I wasn't happy in the marriage. I gathered evidence, but I didn't discuss it with Trudy. I was planning to leave, but I didn't know how to do it. So I read a couple of books on how to change your appearance and obtain new papers. It's not complicated. Just takes a little planning."

"So you grew a beard and gained twenty kilos."

"Yes. I was amazed at how different I looked with the beard. I wasn't happy at work, either. One day I saw a sailboat off the

44

coast, and I desperately wanted to be on it, to sail away to a place where no one knew me. I knew then I'd disappear, but I had to be patient. I couldn't leave Trudy and the baby with nothing, so I bought a two million dollar life insurance plan. I planned my funeral. Then I learned about Mr. Benny Aricia and his lawsuit against the government. All the other partners were involved. I was a partner, too, but they kept their secret from me.

"Suddenly they were sending me on a lot of business trips so they could meet with Aricia without me. But I was making plans, too. When I was in Miami, I found a man who makes false passports and driver's licenses. In Boston, I met someone who helps people disappear. In Ohio, I paid a man to teach me about bugs."

"Tell me about the car crash."

Patrick stood and said, "Let's take a walk. I need to get out of this room."

They walked down the hall and sat looking out a window.

"It was a Sunday—February the ninth," Patrick began. "I found the place for the accident the day before. At about ten o'clock that night, I left the cabin. I stopped at Verhall's Country Store and bought some gas. Three kilometers down the road I turned onto a dirt road and stopped. I put on some protective clothes and drove back to the highway. At the top of a steep hill, I drove off the side of the road.

"I was scared when the car went into the air. It crashed and rolled onto its side. My shoulder hurt, but I was able to climb out. I took off the protective clothes and threw them into the Blazer. Earlier that day, I'd hidden four cans of gasoline. I put three cans inside the car, and poured the gasoline from the fourth can around the inside and outside of the car. Then I stepped back, lit a cigarette, and threw it onto the car. It exploded like a bomb."

He took a drink of soda. "I ran to find the old motorcycle I'd hidden, pushed it up the hill, and rode away. Soon I was back at my cabin. I was scared, but I knew I was running to freedom and a new life. Patrick was dead. It was exciting."

"What about the guy burning in the car, Patrick?" Karl almost asked. Instead he said, "Weren't you afraid Pepper would see you?"

Patrick studied his feet for a few seconds, and then said, "Pepper was gone."

Karl ordered a pizza. After they ate, he said, "You were at the cabin."

"Yes. It was around 11:30. I covered the windows so no one would see the lights. Then I cut my hair and colored it dark brown, and I shaved my beard. I felt like a different person. I cleaned the cabin really well and left at 1 A.M."

"Did you have any concern for Trudy?"

"No. I knew she'd handle the shock well and that she'd be a good widow for about a month. Then she'd get the life insurance money."

"Pepper's gun, tent, and sleeping bag were found under one of the beds. How'd they get there?"

Patrick looked at the wall. "I don't know."

"Where'd you go?" Karl asked.

"To Mobile, Alabama."

"The next morning, you were a new man in a new world. All your worries and problems left behind."

Patrick smiled. He enjoyed telling his story now. "Most of them. It was exciting, and also frightening. I called a taxi, went to a mall, and bought new clothes. I put on my new clothes and looked like a travelling businessman. I took a taxi to the airport, rented a car, and drove to Orange Beach, where I rented an apartment. I watched the evening news and saw that I'd died in the fire after the accident. The next morning, I rented a sailboat. Then I drove to Biloxi and watched my funeral."

♦

The Judge enjoyed the evening so much that he called Patrick the next day to see if they could do it again. Patrick was anxious for company. When he arrived, Karl sat next to Patrick's bed, and they ate the pizza he'd brought.

"Why are you retiring?" Patrick asked.

"How did you know I'm retiring? I haven't told many people, and you were in Brazil."

"I had a spy, Karl."

"Someone here?"

"Of course not. I couldn't risk contacting anyone here. I had an attorney friend there. A woman."

"Now I understand. She's the one who has the money."

Patrick smiled and laughed. "What do you want to know about the money, Karl?"

"Everything. Where is it? How much is left?"

"I can't tell you where it is. There's more money now than I took."

"How'd you do it?"

Patrick walked across the room and stretched. Then he sat down on the edge of the bed. "I got lucky," he whispered. "I was leaving, Karl, with or without the money. I knew the money was coming to the firm, and I had a plan to get it. But, if it didn't work, I was still leaving."

"We got as far as your funeral last night."

"Right. I stayed at Orange Beach a couple of days, listening to Portuguese language tapes. I also listened to conversations I'd recorded around the office, and I organized documents about Aricia. I learned how to sail and then hid in the sailboat and watched Biloxi from there."

"Why did you want to do that?"

"I had the office bugged. I could listen to their conversations on the boat, and I recorded all of them."

"Do you have these tapes?"

47

"Of course. There were hundreds of them. At night I listened to them and organized the important parts. I knew everything that was said in that office. I knew where the money was going and when it would get there."

"So, how'd you steal it?"

"I flew to Miami. Then I used a false passport saying I was Doug Vitrano, flew to Nassau, and went to the bank that the money was being wired to. I was sitting in the manager's office drinking coffee when the wire came in. I immediately had the money wired out, to a bank in Malta, with instructions to wire it onto Panama. When I left the bank, I took a taxi to the airport and flew to New York. I was extremely nervous. I was sure someone would be waiting for me when the plane landed.

"Tell me, Karl," Patrick asked curiously, "when did you hear that the money was missing?"

Karl laughed. "Well, your partners at the firm couldn't keep their settlement quiet. The whole town knew they were going to be very rich. They were buying big Mercedes, new houses, new sailboats. They didn't try to hide it; they wanted people to know.

"You took the money on Thursday, March 26. The next day, I heard there were problems with the big lawsuit at the firm. The money had disappeared."

"Was my name mentioned?"

"Not the first day. It didn't take long, though. The bank's hidden camera had photographed someone looking a little like you. Then people started talking. The FBI came and questioned everyone around here. A week after it happened, we all believed that you'd done it. How long did you stay in New York?"

"About a week. I had the money wired to Canada because I had a Canadian passport now. I studied Portuguese. After three months, I went to Lisbon and studied the language for a couple of months. Then, on August 5, 1992, I flew to São Paulo. I was free. No one would ever find me. I almost cried, Karl. I looked at the people and thought, 'I'm now one of them. I'm a Brazilian named Danilo, and I'll never be anybody else.'"

Chapter 11   Leah's Story

Paulo Miranda's last phone call from his daughter had been two days earlier. She was in a hotel in New Orleans. She was scared, though trying desperately not to show it. He was angry that she wouldn't give more details, and he was worried about her. And he was tired of the men who were following him everywhere he went.

After finishing his work, he walked to his car in the parking lot. He was thinking, his eyes down. A small red van was parked next to his car. As he approached, the driver got out and opened the back door, but Paulo didn't notice. Osmar stopped Paulo and roughly pushed him into the van. The door closed. A gun was pointed between his eyes, and a voice told him to be silent. The van raced away.

An hour and a half later, it stopped behind a farmhouse, and Paulo was led inside. He wouldn't be harmed, he was told, unless he tried to escape. A phone call to the police informed them of the kidnapping. Calls were made to Paulo's son in Rio, to the manager of Eva's apartment, and to one of her friends. The message was the same: Paulo Miranda had been kidnapped, and the police were investigating.

Eva was staying in New York, moving frequently. She called her father, and there was no answer. Then she called her brother and learned about the kidnapping. He was going crazy. No, there hadn't been a request for money.

Against Patrick's specific instructions, she called him, speaking in Portuguese. "Patrick, it's Leah," she said, trying to show no emotion.

"What's wrong?" he asked, in Portuguese. He wasn't pleased to hear her voice.

"It's my father," she said and told him the story of Paulo's disappearance. "I have to go home."

"No, Leah," he said calmly. "It's a trap. They're not asking for money. They want *you*."

She played with her hair and watched the people rushing by. "So what do I do?"

"Go to New Orleans. Call Sandy when you get there."

While she waited at the airport, she thought about her father and the terrible things they could be doing to him. They were hurting him because of her. And there was nothing she could do.

Patrick called Sandy. "She's in serious danger. Be extremely careful when you go to meet her," he said.

An hour later, Sandy left his office and walked around the block three times. When he was certain no one was behind him, he went to Leah's room.

"I'm sorry about your father," he said. "Have you heard anything?"

"No. I've been travelling."

"Who are these people?"

"There's a file on the table," she said, and poured coffee. "Patrick and I met two years ago, in 1994. Patrick said he was a Canadian businessman and needed a lawyer who had experience with international money and banking. But he really needed a friend. I was a friend for two days, and then we fell in love. He told me everything about his past. He'd made a perfect escape, and he had lots of money, but he couldn't forget his past. He had to know who was chasing him, and how close they were.

"In August of 1994, I came to the US and contacted an investigation firm in Atlanta—the Pluto Group. I gave them a false name and told them I needed information about the search for Patrick Lanigan. I paid them 50,000 dollars. They sent people to Biloxi, contacted Patrick's old law firm, and pretended to have information about where he was. The lawyers referred them to Jack Stephano. They met with him in Washington and offered to sell their information. Stephano agreed to pay 50,000 dollars if it led to Patrick. During these meetings, they learned that Stephano believed Patrick was in Brazil. This, of course, frightened Patrick and me.

"I continued to contact the Pluto Group every few months. They were hired to follow Stephano's investigation. They contacted Benny Aricia and the insurance companies with the same story about possible information. They were always referred to Jack Stephano."

"How did Stephano find him?"

"I can't tell you that. Patrick will have to do it."

Sandy thought for a moment. It would be easier if they told him everything so that he, the lawyer, could help them with their future. Maybe they didn't need help.

Leah handed him the file from the table. "These are the people who have my father," she said.

"Stephano?"

"Yes. I'm the only person who knows where the money is, Sandy. The kidnapping is a trap."

"How does Stephano know about you?"

"Patrick told them. You've seen the burns, haven't you?"

Sandy stood. "Then why didn't Patrick tell them where the money is?"

"Because he doesn't know. I have control of it. Now I'm being chased, and my father's caught in the middle."

"What am I supposed to do?"

She opened a drawer and removed another file. "This contains information about the FBI investigation of Patrick. The agent in charge is a man named Cutter, in Biloxi. As soon as I knew Patrick had been captured, I called Cutter. It probably saved

Patrick's life. I told him that Patrick had been found by people working for Jack Stephano. We think the FBI went straight to him and threatened him. His people in Brazil tortured Patrick for a few hours, almost killed him, and then gave him to the FBI."

Sandy listened with his eyes closed tight. "Go on," he said.

"Two days later, Stephano was arrested in Washington."

"How do you know this?"

"I'm still paying a lot of money to the Pluto Group. We suspect that Stephano's talking to the FBI, while at the same time he's quietly following me. And my father."

"What am I supposed to tell Cutter?"

"First, tell him about me. Tell him that I'm making decisions for Patrick and I know everything. Then, tell him about my father."

◆

When Dr. Hayani looked into Patrick's room in the morning, Patrick was sitting in a chair by the window, looking at the closed curtains. "Patrick, are you OK?" he asked.

After a minute Patrick answered, "I'm fine, Doc. But I didn't sleep at all."

"You're safe now, Patrick. The sun's up."

When he left, Patrick got up and walked to the door.

"Did you sleep well?" the guard at the door asked, as he did every morning.

"I slept safe, Eddie, thanks," Patrick said, as he did every morning. He returned to his room and did some exercises.

The routine was the same every day. He wanted to be Danilo again, with his quiet life in his small house. He wanted to walk along the streets of Ponta Pora and run in the country. He missed Brazil. And he missed Eva—her soft touch, her beautiful smile. He couldn't live without her. He'd escaped before. Why couldn't he escape again? He'd have a perfect life with Eva. He'd put her in danger, and now he must protect her. Could he do it again? Or had his luck ended?

♦

Sandy met Cutter at 8 A.M.

"Do you remember that phone call you received thirteen days ago?" Sandy asked. "The lady from Brazil?" Cutter said he did, and Sandy continued, "I've met with her a few times. She's a lawyer for Patrick." He quickly explained most of what he knew about Leah, though he never mentioned her name. Then he asked about the Stephano investigation.

Cutter became cautious. "How do you know about that?"

"The lady from Brazil knows all about Stephano. Remember, she gave you his name. He's still trying to get my client, and I'd like to stop him."

"And how do you know this?"

"Because his men in Brazil have kidnapped the woman's father."

Cutter's mouth opened, and he looked at the ceiling. Then it made sense. "Does she know where the money is?"

"That's a possibility. The kidnapping is an effort to make her go back to Brazil. Then they'll capture her and treat her like they treated Patrick. It's all about money."

"There's not much we can do about it."

"Yes, there is. Put pressure on Stephano. Tell him the woman isn't going to be trapped, that she's preparing to go to the Brazilian police with the name of Jack Stephano."

"I'll see what I can do." Cutter hadn't forgotten the fact that Sandy had filed a several million dollar lawsuit against the FBI for crimes it didn't commit.

"Stephano only cares about the money," Sandy said. "If the old man gets hurt, Stephano will never see any of it. Tell him to release the old man. Then we might talk about the money."

53

♦

Patrick walked around one end of the doctors' conference room while Sandy sat and listened. "Things are changing, Sandy," Patrick said without looking at him. "We have to move fast. She won't stay here while her father's missing."

"As usual, I'm confused. But I'm just the lawyer. Why should I know anything?"

"She has the files and records, and the story. There's a beach house at Perdido. She's waiting for you there."

"And I'm supposed to change all my plans and race over there right now," Sandy said angrily. "I have other clients. I have court this afternoon. My daughter's got soccer."

"I'm sorry, Sandy. I couldn't know about a kidnapping. Try and understand."

Sandy took a deep breath. "What might we discuss at the beach house?"

"Aricia."

♦

Sandy parked in front of the beach house. Leah answered the door with a smile. On the table was a box, and beside it were papers neatly arranged. "This is the Aricia file," Leah said. "Patrick prepared it."

They sat at a small table in the kitchen and ate.

"How's Patrick?" she asked.

"Patrick's OK. The burns are getting better." He ate a bit. "I'm sorry. I forgot to ask about your father."

"I talked to my brother today, and there's still no word. It's difficult. I can't go home, and I can't stay here."

"I'm very sorry, Leah." He asked more questions—general questions, not about the kidnapping—as he ate. She didn't touch her food.

When he finished, they moved to the table with the box and papers on it. "How much do you know about the Aricia matter?" she asked.

"Just the information that was in the paper."

"These documents and tapes are the evidence for everything I'm going to tell you. The Aricia claim was false from the beginning." She spoke slowly. "Benny Aricia made the plan to cheat both his company and his government. He was helped by some very good lawyers—Patrick's old firm—and a senator, Bogan's cousin, in Washington.

"Patrick was a new partner then. He wasn't included in the Aricia plan, but he knew something was happening. He found out that the secrecy was because of Aricia, and he was patient. He pretended to notice nothing, but he was gathering evidence. A lot of it's in this box."

"Explain how the claim was false."

"Aricia ran New Coastal Shipyards in Pascagoula. It's a small division of Platt & Rockland."

"I know all that. They have big defense contracts and are known for cheating the government."

"That's right. New Coastal was working on an enormous building program for the Navy. Aricia wrote false work records, claiming thousands of hours for work that was never done, for employees who never existed. He charged unbelievably high prices for materials—drinking cups for thirty dollars each, for example. He created piles of paperwork, very little with his name on it. He kept good records, which he later gave to his lawyers. They would file the lawsuit with the government, and Aricia would get the reward."

"And Patrick got the records." Sandy looked at the box. "And this has been hidden since he disappeared."

"Yes. Patrick always knew he'd be caught."

Sandy had lots of questions, but he told himself to relax. "So

Aricia's plan worked. Did Bogan know Aricia had caused the overcharges?"

"Yes." She pointed to the box. "This box is full of tapes of their conversations."

They loaded the whole Aricia file into the trunk of his car and said good-bye. She promised to call him within twenty-four hours.

Chapter 12   Stephano's Story—Continued

The third day, Underhill was back. "We'll start where we stopped yesterday, Mr. Stephano. Your arrival in Brazil."

"Right. It's a big country and has a history of being a great place to hide. We put together a file on Lanigan and had it translated into Portuguese. We had computer artists make pictures of his appearance. Then we hurried to Brazil and hired the best investigators we could find. In April 1994, we found the doctor who'd changed Lanigan's chin and nose. We knew then that he was in Brazil."

♦

Stephano's fourth meeting began early. The questioner was a new one, Oliver.

"You were talking about the doctor who changed Lanigan's chin and nose," Oliver said. "Continue."

Stephano got comfortable in his chair. "For a long time we didn't find anything. Then, late in '94, we were contacted by an investigation firm in Atlanta—the Pluto Group. They said they might have some information I'd want. They had a mysterious client who claimed to know something about Lanigan. Obviously, I was interested. The client, not surprisingly, wanted lots of money. This was encouraging. If their client expected a big reward, then the client knew that Lanigan still had plenty of money. In July of '95, the Pluto Group approached me and said their client could lead us to a place in Brazil where Lanigan had recently lived. We agreed on the sum of 50,000 dollars. After the money was wired to a bank in Panama, I was given an address of an apartment building in the small city of Itajaí. We showed the manager our pictures of Patrick. He said the man's name was Jan Horst, a German who'd rented an apartment for two months."

"What about the Pluto Group?"

"We didn't hear much from them for six months. Then, in January of this year, they returned. Their client needed money and was ready to tell us everything. For a few million dollars we could learn exactly where our man was. But their client wouldn't talk until the money was paid, and I wouldn't pay until their client talked. Eventually, another suggestion was made. For 50,000 dollars we would get the name of a place where Lanigan had lived after he left Itajaí. We agreed because it would tell us whether their client had good information."

"Where was the second town?"

"São Mateus, a small town with friendly people. We spent a month there showing our pictures. The apartment manager recognized him as Derrick Boone, a British man. We didn't learn anything more, so we left São Mateus in early March and decided to concentrate on the smaller towns near São Paulo and Rio. The Pluto Group still wanted a million dollars, and my client wouldn't pay without being certain that the information was good."

"Did you ever learn how their client knew so much about Lanigan's movements?"

"No. One theory was that their client was also chasing Lanigan, for an unknown reason. The second theory, and the most likely, was that their client was someone Lanigan knew and trusted. My client and I decided we couldn't allow the opportunity to escape."

"How did you reach an agreement?"

"In August of this year, they made another offer: recent photos of Lanigan, in exchange for another 50,000 dollars. We said yes. The money was wired, and they handed me the photos in my office."

"Could I see them, please?"

"Sure." Stephano pulled them from his case. The first was Lanigan in a crowded market; he wore dark glasses. The second was taken as he walked along a sidewalk; he looked no different from any Brazilian. The third was Patrick washing his Volkswagen; the dark glasses were off, and it was a clear photo of his face.

"We agreed to pay the million dollars. The money was placed in an account in Geneva. Their client gave us the name of the town, and the street address where he lived. We raced there and found him. His name was Danilo Silva. Then we watched him for a week. We had to be patient. If we made one bad move, the police would be told and would protect him. So we waited and planned. We finally captured him outside of town, on a small road with no witnesses, and took him to a house in Paraguay."

♦

Underhill joined Oliver after a coffee break. "We've seen the photos of the burns, Mr. Stephano. And we, the FBI, have been sued for the injuries caused by your men. Now tell us how you did it."

"I wasn't there. I knew he'd be given electric shocks. I had no idea it would cause serious burns."

Underhill and Oliver looked at each other in disbelief and whispered. They both asked a number of questions about the capture and questioning. Finally, they asked the most important question. "During the questioning of Mr. Lanigan, what did you learn about the money?"

58

"Not much. He told us where the money had been, but it had been moved. The man who did the questioning believes that Mr. Lanigan didn't know where the money was."

"Did Mr. Lanigan mention a partner?"

"I don't know."

They whispered again and then paused. Stephano waited nervously. Then the door opened, and Hamilton Jaynes walked in, followed by Warren. "I've been listening in the next room," Jaynes said with a smile. "And suddenly I wonder if you're being truthful."

Stephano was more anxious. "Of course I am."

"Of course. Have you ever heard the name Eva Miranda? She's a lawyer in Rio. A friend of Patrick's."

"No."

"Well, that's what bothers me, Jack. I think you know exactly who she is. You're trying to find her."

"I don't know what you're talking about," Stephano said weakly.

Underhill spoke. "He's lying." Oliver and Warren agreed.

Jaynes picked up a sheet of paper. "This is a story from a Rio paper this morning. It tells of the kidnapping of Mr. Paulo Miranda. His daughter is Patrick's friend, Jack. We've checked with the police in Rio. Nothing has been heard from the kidnappers. So where's Mr. Miranda?"

"I don't know what you're talking about."

Jaynes looked at the other end of the table. "Still lying," Underhill said, and Oliver and Warren agreed.

"We had an agreement, Jack. You'd tell us the truth. We'd drop the charges against you, and we wouldn't arrest your clients. Now what am I supposed to do, Jack?"

Stephano looked at Underhill and Oliver. "She knows where the money is," he said quietly.

"Do you know where she is?"

"No. She left Rio when we found Patrick. We haven't found her."

Jaynes looked at his men. Yes, Stephano had stopped lying. "Leave the girl alone, Jack. And release her father."

"I'll think about it."

"No. You'll do it now."

Chapter 13 Eva

Leah didn't see the man at the supermarket at first, but then she turned and saw his green eyes staring at her. She calmly walked away. Minutes later, she saw him again, hiding his face but watching every move she made.

She was frightened, but remained calm as she walked through the store. She saw him once more in the store, and then saw him walking through the parking lot, carrying nothing. She paid for her groceries as calmly as possible, but her hands shook as she took her change.

She got in her car and drove in the direction of the beach house, though she knew she could never go back there. After a kilometer, she turned quickly and saw him three cars behind her. She desperately wanted to see Patrick so she could scream at him. This was not part of their agreement.

She drove on, remaining calm as Patrick had taught her. The man with the green eyes wasn't following her now, but she knew others would be watching. An hour later, she entered the airport in Pensacola and bought a ticket for the next flight, which went to Miami.

In Miami, she bought a one-way ticket to São Paulo. Why not visit her country? The agent at the passport checkpoint had seen an announcement that the FBI was looking for a young Brazilian woman, age thirty-one, and pushed an alarm. A manager appeared and said, "Could you step in here, Ms. Pires?" He pointed to a row of doors.

"Is there a problem?" she demanded as they walked.

"Not really. Just a few questions." When they entered a small room, he asked about her reason for going to São Paulo. Then he asked, "Where's your baggage? According to our records, you entered the country eight days ago. Eight days, and no baggage. Seems odd, doesn't it?"

"Is it a crime to travel without baggage?" she asked.

"No, but it is a crime to use a false passport in the US. Do you know a person by the name of Eva Miranda?"

Leah's heart stopped, her face fell, and she knew the chase was at an end.

◆

The long table was piled with papers and files, and the Aricia box sat empty in a corner. Patrick and Sandy were looking through the files when Cutter walked in.

"I thought you'd want to know that we have Eva Miranda. We caught her at the airport in Miami, on her way to Brazil."

Patrick stopped, shocked. "Where is she?" he asked.

"In jail, in Miami. Just thought you'd want to know," Cutter said with a smile, and left.

Patrick sat down. At least Stephano and Aricia hadn't caught her; she was safe with the FBI. But he couldn't believe she was returning to Brazil without him.

"She was fine when I left her," Sandy said. "She didn't mention Miami or Brazil. She told me she rented the beach house for a month."

"Then she got scared. Find a lawyer in Miami, Sandy. And quickly. She must be extremely scared."

◆

Eva had never been in jail before. She thought about her father and prayed that they weren't hurting him. And she prayed for Patrick. She found comfort in the money. Tomorrow she'd demand a good attorney. She'd be released soon and would be home to find her father. She'd hide somewhere in Rio; it would be simple. This was a safe place, she decided. The men who hurt Patrick and now had her father couldn't touch her. She knew the FBI would tell Patrick that they had her, and he'd have a plan.

♦

Sandy called Mark Birck, a criminal lawyer he knew in Miami. At nine the next morning, Birck was at the jail.

"Patrick sent me," he told Leah. "Are you OK?"

"I'm fine. Thanks for coming. When will I be released?"

"Not for a few days. Patrick's very concerned about you."

"I know. Tell him I'm fine. And I'm very concerned about him."

"Now, Patrick wants a detailed account of exactly how you were caught."

She smiled and relaxed. Of course Patrick wanted details.

Chapter 14   Settlements

At first Bogan and Vitrano were happy when Patrick was found, but soon it became obvious that the money wasn't following him back to Biloxi. Then they remembered the bugs Stephano had discovered in their office. They'd forgotten about Patrick's tapes. Now they were worried. Too much had been said in the offices.

"Do you think we'll get the money?" Vitrano asked.

"No." There was a long pause. "We'll be lucky if we're not indicted."

♦

Sandy went to Parrish's office at 10 A.M. Parrish had asked for the meeting. There was a lot of missing information about the murder, and he wanted it. What was the cause of death? And the big question, who was killed?

After a short discussion, Parrish said, "I have a suggestion: If your client gives me information, I can reduce his crime to accidental killing instead of capital murder. The penalty is twenty years in prison. Would he consider this?"

"Go do it. Then we'll talk."

Sandy returned to his room at the Biloxi Nugget Hotel, which he'd organized as his office. His first visitor was J. Murray Riddleton, Trudy's lawyer. Riddleton gave Sandy their suggested divorce settlement. They knew it would be changed to whatever Patrick wanted.

The second visitor was Talbot Mims, the Biloxi lawyer for Northern Case. "Do you know Jack Stephano?" Sandy asked. Mims said he didn't. "I didn't think so. He's an investigator hired by Aricia, Northern Case, and Monarch-Sierra to find Patrick. Look at these," Sandy said with a smile as he slid a set of photos of Patrick's burns across the table to Mims.

"These were in the paper when you sued the FBI."

"The FBI didn't find Patrick. We sued them to make people feel sympathetic toward Patrick. Anyway, the men responsible for these injuries were working for Stephano. Northern Case was one of his clients."

Mims hid his surprise. "Can you prove this?" he asked calmly. "What do you want?"

"The FBI can prove it. I want to talk to someone with the power to make decisions. Tomorrow at 4 P.M."

"We'll be here," Mims said, and left in a rush.

Hal Ladd, working for Monarch-Sierra, arrived in the afternoon. Sandy repeated the questions, information, and demands.

When Ladd left, Sandy went to a coffee shop to meet Cutter. "We need to have a serious talk," he said. "I can prove that the Aricia claim against Platt & Rockland was completely false, that he hired the Bogan firm to cheat the government, and that he had help from a senator."

"There's still the matter of the dead body." Cutter drank his coffee, and then said, "What kind of proof?"

"Documents, recorded phone calls."

Cutter stared at Sandy. "Patrick gathered the evidence before he disappeared. And now he wants to make an agreement with us. But what about the murder?"

"That's a state matter, not really your concern."

"Let me talk to the people in Washington."

♦

The following morning, after a phone call from Cutter, Jaynes and several people from his office, Parrish, and Mast, the US Attorney for the district, met Sandy in his hotel room office. Two court reporters were also present. No one smiled, but they weren't unhappy to be there.

Sandy gave greetings from his client and discussed the charges against Patrick. "The government charges are serious, but they're small in comparison to capital murder. We'd like you to drop them so we can concentrate on the murder charge. We have an offer that includes money."

"We have no claim to the money," Jaynes said. "It wasn't stolen from the government."

"That's where you're wrong." Sandy explained how Aricia had worked with Bogan's firm to cheat the government out of 600 million dollars. He told them about the documents and tapes. Then he said, "Here's our suggestion. We'll hand over the documents and tapes. Patrick will return the money, all of it. In exchange, the government will drop its charges. His Brazilian attorney, Eva Miranda, must be released immediately." Jaynes looked at the floor. "And it has to be done today," Sandy added, "or my client will keep the money, destroy the evidence, and spend his time in prison."

"Let's talk about this," said Sprawling, one of the government officials with Jaynes.

"Great idea," Sandy said, as he put a tape in the tape player. "The date was January 14, 1992," he said. And he played a conversation between Bogan, Vitrano, and Aricia that mentioned the senator's cooperation. "Gentlemen, this is just one example," he told them when it finished.

The others left the room to talk. It soon became obvious to Mast that the rest had already made their decision. "So, we're going to accept it," he said, acting as if he didn't care.

"Yes," Sprawling said. "We look good by getting the money back. Patrick stays in jail for a long time. We arrest more important criminals."

The group returned to Sandy's office, and Sprawling spoke for them. "About the money, how much is your client willing to return?" he asked Sandy.

"All ninety million."

"The government wants all of it plus 9 percent."

"We'll give 3 percent extra, making a total of 113 million."

"We're concerned about the lawsuit you filed," Sprawling said.

"We'll drop the charges against the FBI," Sandy said, "but I need Jaynes to do something for us. We'll discuss it later."

"All right. When can your client come before the grand jury?"

"Whenever you need him."

"When would you like Ms. Miranda to be released?"

"Tomorrow. Anything else?"

"Nothing from the government," Sprawling said.

"Good. Here's what I suggest," Sandy said. "We've already prepared a settlement agreement and an order to drop the lawsuit. You can sign it, I'll take it to my client, and within a couple of hours we'll be finished."

◆

Mrs. Stephano was sleeping well again. The FBI had left their street, and the neighbors had stopped calling. Her husband was relaxed. Then, at 5:30 A.M., the phone rang.

"Who's calling?" she demanded when she picked it up.

"Hamilton Jaynes, FBI."

"Oh, my God!" she said. "Jack, it's the FBI again."

Stephano took the phone.

"Good morning, Jack. This is Hamilton Jaynes. I wanted to let you know that we've got the girl, Eva Miranda. She's safe, so you can tell your men to stop looking for her."

Stephano sat up. Their last hope was gone. The search for the money was finally over. "Congratulations," he said.

"Look, Jack, I've sent some men to Rio. You have twenty-four hours to release her father. If he's not free by then, I'll arrest you and Aricia, and probably Mr. Atterson at Monarch-Sierra and Mr. Jill at Northern Case."

"I hear you." And the phone went quiet.

Mrs. Stephano was in the bathroom with the door locked, too frightened to face him. Stephano went to the kitchen and made coffee. He was tired of Benny Aricia. He waited an hour and then called him.

When Stephano called, Benny knew his dream was over. He'd hoped to find the money and then disappear with it, just like Patrick. But he still had a million dollars, and he had friends in other countries. It was time to leave, just like Patrick.

He and Guy left Biloxi after dark. Guy went to Mobile, and Benny went to New Orleans. He watched closely as he drove, but didn't see anyone behind him. He went to the airport and flew to Chicago. Then onto New York at dawn.

The FBI was in Boca Raton, Florida, watching Benny's home. His Swedish girlfriend was still there. She'd leave soon, they thought, and it would be much easier to follow her.

♦

It was almost dark when Paulo, his eyes covered, was led from the house. When the car stopped, he was helped from the back. A voice said, "To your left, 300 meters, is a farmhouse with a telephone. Go there for help. I have a gun. If you turn around, I'll have to kill you."

Paulo's body shook as the man uncovered his eyes and said, "Walk forward quickly."

Paulo walked to the farmhouse and called the police. Then he called his son.

In Miami, Mark Birck delivered to Eva the news that her father had been released and hadn't been harmed.

♦

Patrick called Karl and invited him for lunch. They sat outside and ate sandwiches.

"I hear they caught your lady friend in Miami," Karl said.

"Yes. But she'll be out of jail soon. Just a small problem with her passport."

Karl ate a bite of his sandwich. He was getting used to long silences in their conversations.

Finally Patrick said, "Have you ever been to Brazil?"

"No."

"You should go sometime. The land's beautiful, and the people are gentle. It's my home, Karl. I can't wait to go back there. I'm not Patrick now. Patrick's dead. He was trapped in a bad life, fat, and unhappy. I'm Danilo Silva, a much happier person with a quiet life in another country."

"Listen, Patrick. I think it's time for me to give your case to

Judge Trussel. I've done all I can to help you. I've told him about your awful injuries and how important it is for you to stay here as long as possible. He understands. But you have to realize that at some time you're going to be put in jail. And you might be there for a long time."

"Do you think I killed that boy, Karl?"

Karl put the rest of his sandwich down. "It looks that way. First, there were parts of a human body in the car, so somebody was killed. Second, the FBI has investigated everyone who disappeared around February 9, 1992. Pepper is the only person within 450 kilometers who hasn't been heard from."

"Do you think I killed him? Do you think I could kill someone?"

"No. But your recent history is full of surprises."

Patrick returned to his room, and Sandy arrived a few minutes later. "We did it!" He threw the agreement on Patrick's worktable. "We got everything we wanted."

"How much money?" When Sandy told him, Patrick closed his eyes. That was a lot of his fortune, but there was plenty left; enough for him and Eva to settle down somewhere safe one day and have a large house full of kids. He signed the agreement, and Sandy raced back to the hotel.

At 2 P.M., Talbot Mims and a manager from Northern Case arrived at the hotel. Sandy took them to his office. Hal Ladd and a lawyer from Monarch-Sierra joined them. Sandy repeated the information about Patrick's torture and reminded them that Stephano was working for three clients: Benny Aricia and their two companies.

"How do you plan to prove this?" asked Mims.

Sandy opened a door and asked Jaynes to join them. With great pleasure, Jaynes described the things Stephano had told them about the search for Patrick, the capture, and the torture. All done with money provided by Aricia and the two insurance companies.

"Any questions for Mr. Jaynes?" Sandy asked happily when Jaynes finished. There were none. Both companies were rich, and neither company wanted this problem.

"Here's the agreement," Sandy said. "First, Northern Case is trying to recover the 2.5 million paid to Trudy Lanigan. We prefer that you drop the lawsuit. Besides, most of the money has been spent. If you do this, my client will drop his claim for personal injuries against your company."

"Is that all?" Mims asked, not believing it.

"Yes. That's it."

"OK. We agree."

Sandy gave them their settlement agreement and asked them to leave so he could talk with Ladd and his client.

"Your settlement's a bit different," he told them. "You paid Stephano twice as much as they did. And you have a lot more cash than Northern Case."

"How much do you have in mind?" Cohen, the Monarch-Sierra lawyer, asked anxiously.

"Nothing for Patrick. He's very concerned, however, about the child. She's six, and her mother spends money quickly. Patrick would like a quarter of a million to go into a special account for her, money that her mother can't use. Plus, he wants the same amount to pay his legal costs. Total of half a million, paid very quietly so your client won't be embarrassed by those pictures of his injuries."

The company was anxious to finish. "We'll do it," Cohen said.

Sandy handed him copies of their settlement agreement and left.

♦

At eight that evening, Sandy visited Patrick. "It's all done," he said, as he handed Patrick a pile of paperwork. "We gave the documents and tapes to the FBI an hour ago."

Patrick took the settlement agreements and read them carefully before signing them. "Good work, Sandy."

"We had a good day. Tomorrow we'll finish with Trudy. It's too bad the dead body is in your way."

Patrick stepped to the window, his back to the room. The curtains and the window were open.

Sandy watched him. "You have to tell me sometime, Patrick," he said. "Why don't we start with Pepper?"

"OK. I didn't kill Pepper."

"Was Pepper alive when you disappeared?"

Patrick shut the window, closed the curtains, and sat on his bed. Then he said in a quiet voice, "I knew Pepper. He came to the cabin asking for food in December of '91. He told me he lived in the woods most of the time. He was very shy. I cooked for him and asked about his family. He said he hadn't been home in two weeks.

"A couple of weeks later, he came again. I cooked and we ate. He said he'd had a fight with his mother. He hated her. When I told him I was a lawyer, he told me about his legal problems. At his last job some money was missing, and they blamed Pepper. He didn't take it. It was another very good reason to stay in the woods. I said I'd help him."

"And your plan began."

"Something like that. We saw each other a few more times in the woods. I told Pepper the police were going to arrest him soon. This was a lie, but he was scared. I suggested disappearing. He liked the idea of going to the mountains in the West. I got him a new name, a new driver's license, and a passport. On Sunday, February 9—"

"The date of your 'death.'"

"Yes. I drove Pepper to the bus station in Jackson. He was excited. I told him he could never come back. I gave him 2,000 dollars and left him."

"His gun, tent, and sleeping bag were found in the cabin."

"I wanted them to think Pepper burned in the car."

"Where is he now?"

"I don't know."

Sandy was angry. "If I ask a question, I deserve an answer. Why can't you tell me everything?"

"Because you don't need to know everything."

Sandy picked up the settlements. "I'm tired. I'll be back tomorrow, and you'll tell me everything."

Chapter 15   Final Arrangements

Eva walked out of jail at 8:30 A.M. Mark Birck rushed her to his car and took her to the airport, where a small jet was waiting to take her to New York. He told her that from New York she'd go to London.

Eva closed her eyes and thought of Patrick. Then she noticed the car phone and asked to use it. She called her father in Brazil and had a tearful conversation. She promised to be home soon. Her legal work in the United States was almost finished, and she missed her home.

In New York, the people at the British Airways check-in counter looked at her questioningly because she had no baggage. She fought to control her nerves. She couldn't be arrested again. She loved Patrick, but this was too much.

In the lounge she had coffee and called Sandy.

"Are you OK?" he asked.

"I'm fine, Sandy. I'm at JFK, on my way to London. How's Patrick?"

"Wonderful. We've made a settlement with the government people—113 million." Sandy waited for her to say something.

"When?" was all she said.

"I'll have instructions when you get to London. Call me when you get to the hotel."

"Tell Patrick I still love him, even after going to jail."

♦

Later in the morning, Sandy met with Riddleton to look over the divorce settlement agreement. Trudy had already signed it, and Riddleton didn't want to see her again.

"We'll sign it," Sandy said. "There's a new arrangement involving your client and her lawsuit with Northern Case. They're going to drop their lawsuit against Trudy."

Riddleton's mouth opened. Sandy gave him a copy of the Northern Case Insurance settlement agreement, which he read curiously. "What a pleasant surprise."

"There's one other thing." Sandy told him about the special account that had 250,000 dollars for Ashley Nicole.

"Anything else?" Riddleton asked with a broad smile.

"That's it. The divorce is finished."

♦

Patrick was taken into the courthouse through a side door. He wore new clothes that Sandy had bought. He was pale and thin, but seemed to have no difficulty walking. Actually, Patrick felt great. He entered the courtroom, smiling, and sat at his table. He was relaxed because he knew that this jury couldn't do anything to him.

He talked about the law firm and told the story of Benny Aricia and how he'd gathered his evidence. The jury listened with great interest for two hours. After a short break, some of the taped conversations were played, and they listened for three more hours.

The grand jury voted to indict Benny Aricia, Charles Bogan, Doug Vitrano, Jimmy Havarac, and Ethan Rapley for planning to cheat the government under the False Claims Act. Jaynes and Sprawling returned to Washington.

Before dawn the next morning, officers arrived at the homes of the law firm partners and arrested them. They were taken to jail, but released immediately because of their connections with several judges.

♦

Patrick began, "I had a car wreck case once. The driver was killed, and two people were injured. It was the truck's fault, Sandy, but the driver claimed that our client's car was speeding. We found a witness—Mr. Clovis Goodman, age eighty-one. He tried to help the injured people in the car but couldn't. He left without saying anything to anyone. Later we found him, but he was still too upset to talk about it.

"Clovis lived alone in the country, and I asked if I could visit him. He was a lonely old man who didn't trust lawyers. We drank coffee and talked about everything except the wreck. When I asked about it, he informed me softly that he was there, but he couldn't talk about it yet.

"I went back and we exchanged more stories. I took him to dinner, and we stopped for a few beers. But he still couldn't talk about the wreck. After a month, I put pressure on him. I told him we'd reached an important point in the lawsuit, and it was time for him to answer some questions. He said he was ready. He had tears in his eyes and wanted to help the family in the car. They weren't speeding. We went to trial, and Clovis Goodman was the best witness I've ever seen. The jury gave our clients 2.3 million dollars.

"We became friends. When he got sick and couldn't live by himself, I moved him into a nursing home and took care of his finances. At that time, I was his only friend. He hadn't heard from his relatives for years.

"He got very sick in January of '92. I moved him to a hospital and visited every day. On February 6 he died."

Sandy breathed heavily and closed his eyes tightly. "Clovis wasn't buried, was he?" he asked

"No. I put his body in a freezer at my cabin." Sandy was shocked. "I didn't kill anybody, Sandy. I needed a body, but he was already dead when his body burned."

Sandy walked around the room, then leaned on the wall. "Let's hear the rest of it," he said. "I'm sure you have everything planned."

"I've had time to think about it, yes. There's a Mississippi law about destroying a dead body. It's the only one they can use on me. The penalty is one year in jail. If that's all they can use, Parrish will try very hard to get that."

"He can't let you walk away without any punishment."

"No, he can't. But he won't know about Clovis unless I tell him, and I have to tell him before he'll drop the murder charges. But I'm the only witness, and there's no way to prove the burned body was Clovis."

"So what's the plan?"

"You go to Clovis's granddaughter, tell her the truth, and offer money. We make a settlement with her quietly, and, to get the money, she agrees to tell Parrish not to charge me."

Sandy walked around again, thinking. "We have to give Parrish something," he said. "It's not just him. It's the system, Patrick. If you aren't punished, then you've bought your way out of jail. Everybody else looks bad."

"Then I'll say I'm guilty of destroying Clovis's dead body. I'll go to court and pay money, but no jail time. I'll be free. No one in Brazil will care."

Sandy stopped walking and sat on the bed beside Patrick. "So you'll go back to Brazil?"

"It's home, Sandy."

"And the girl?"

"We'll either have ten kids, or eleven. We haven't decided."

"How much money will you have?"

"Millions. You have to get me out of here, Sandy. I have another life to live."

◆

Sandy visited Clovis's granddaughter at the coffee shop where she worked. "I have good news for you," he said. They sat at a table and had coffee. As efficiently as possible, he told her Patrick's story. She found it amusing.

"Give him the death penalty," she said.

"He didn't kill anybody. The body in the car was already dead. He just stole it. The body was Clovis Goodman, your grandfather."

She looked at him with narrow eyes. "He burned Clovis! Why?"

"He had to have a dead body. Clovis was his client and friend." She looked confused. "It's a crime to destroy a dead body. That means Clovis's family can sue my client."

She smiled and said, "Now I understand."

Sandy smiled, too. "Yes. That's why I'm here. My client would like to make a very quiet settlement with you."

"How much? What's the most you'll pay?"

Sandy drank his coffee. "Fifty thousand."

"OK." They shook hands. Sandy gave her a settlement agreement to sign and wrote a check.

◆

Eva left her London hotel and took a long walk. She looked in the store windows and then stopped for lunch. She listened to the happy people who had no idea who she was. They didn't care. She felt more like Leah Pires than Eva Miranda. She began shopping, without paying attention to the prices. She was a very wealthy woman at the moment.

At two o'clock in the afternoon, she had a meeting with the manager of DeutscheBank's London office. His bank would wire 113 million from its Zurich office to its Washington office, following her instructions.

After the wire, there would be 1.9 million dollars in the account. Another Swiss account had 3 million. A bank on Grand Cayman held 6.5 million. A financial advisor in Bermuda had 4 million. And 7.2 million was in Luxembourg.

♦

The Swedish lady left Benny Aricia's home and put her baggage in his BMW. She sped away, went to the airport, and took a plane to London. When she landed, the officials were watching for her. She took a taxi to her hotel and was delayed at the front desk until the manager was told that the bug had been placed in the phone in her room.

As soon as she went into her room, she called Benny. She told him she was scared but didn't think she'd been followed. They made arrangements to meet at a coffee shop in an hour. She waited there, but Benny didn't come.

The next morning, she read all the newspapers in the hotel. On an inside page of the *Daily Mail* she finally found a two-paragraph story about the capture of an American criminal, Benny Aricia. She packed her bags and took a plane to Sweden.

♦

Patrick was rushed through the back door of the courthouse and into Karl's office. His wounds were still bandaged, and he wore his hospital clothes to remind people that he was hospitalized, not in jail like a criminal.

"I spent two hours with Judge Trussel this morning," Karl said.

"I told him that, in my opinion, this isn't a capital murder trial."

"There's not going to be a trial, Karl. Remember the Hoover trial? A truck hit a car, killing the driver and injuring two passengers. My first trial in your courtroom."

"Of course," Huskey said, relaxing at his desk.

Patrick told him the Clovis story.

When he finished, they sat silently for a few minutes. Then Karl said, "I hear the government's dropped all charges against you."

"That's correct. I talked to the grand jury yesterday. It was great fun, Karl, finally telling all the secrets I've been keeping for years."

"So, the divorce is settled. The government's dropped all charges, and you've agreed to pay back a total of 113 million. The capital murder trial won't happen because there wasn't a murder. The lawsuits filed by the insurance companies have been dropped. Pepper's still alive. That just leaves the charge of destroying a dead body. A small crime." Karl admired his thin friend. He'd talk to Judge Trussel again.

♦

Patrick sat at the end of the table with Sandy on his right and Parrish on his left. Since the government charges had been dropped, Parrish felt pressured to get justice from Patrick for the state.

"You can forget murder, Terry," Patrick said. "I didn't kill anyone. The person in the car had been dead for four days."

Parrish questioned him and accepted that Patrick was right. But he wasn't going to give up completely. "Looks like a year in jail," he said. "A year in Parchman should be good for you."

"Sure, except that I'm not going to Parchman. You don't have a body. You have no idea who was burned, and I'm not telling until we make an agreement. Drop the charges. You can't win."

77

"The family of the dead person doesn't want to sue Patrick," Sandy said.

"You can't prove anything against me. There are no witnesses, and the evidence isn't good enough."

"You can't make us look like fools," Parrish said. "Give us something."

"I'll say I'm guilty of destroying the dead body. But I get no jail time. You can explain to the judge that the family doesn't want to sue me. You can talk about the torture and what I've been through. You can do all that, Parrish, and you'll look very good. But no jail."

Parrish thought for a minute. "And you'll tell us the name of the dead person?"

"I will, but only after we have an agreement."

"OK, but I have to speak with Judge Trussel. He'll have to agree, too."

Patrick smiled at Sandy. Parrish stood up to leave. "Oh, I almost forgot," the District Attorney said. "What can you tell us about Pepper Scarboro?"

"I can give you his new name and passport number."

◆

Sandy, Parrish, and Judge Trussel spent several hours working out a plea agreement to reduce the charges against Patrick. Sandy took it to him at the hospital. They read the agreement aloud, and Patrick signed. Sandy noticed that he was already packing.

Back in his hotel room office, Sandy's phone rang. It was Jack Stephano, who was downstairs and wanted to talk. "I'm here out of curiosity," he told Sandy when he arrived in the office.

"Have they caught Aricia?" Sandy asked.

"Yes. Just hours ago. In London. I'm not working for him any more. I was hired to find the money. I tried, I got paid, and that's finished. But I'm extremely curious about something. We only found Lanigan in Brazil after someone gave us information about him. Someone who knew him well—his movements, his habits, his false names. It was planned by someone very smart. It has to be the girl, right? One of these days, if you learn the truth, I'd like to know. I won't sleep well until I know if she took our money."

◆

The hearing was scheduled for five o'clock in the courthouse. Patrick put on new pants and a large white shirt. He shook hands with Hayani and thanked him for his friendship. After two weeks as a patient and prisoner, Patrick left the hospital. His lawyer was at his side, and his guards followed behind.

It was supposed to be a secret hearing to complete the secret agreements, but people heard about it. In less than thirty minutes, half the city knew, and the courtroom was crowded.

Patrick smiled for the photographers as he was led to the jury room. Karl entered and asked the guards to wait in the hall. "When are you leaving?" he asked.

"I don't know. Soon."

"Can I go with you?"

"Would you really leave? If you had the chance to disappear right now, would you do it?"

"No, I wouldn't leave. But I don't blame you."

"Everybody wants to disappear, Karl. At some time in life, everybody thinks about walking away. Problems can be left behind."

Judge Trussel entered the courtroom. Patrick was led through the door and stood next to Sandy in front of the Judge. He didn't look at his audience.

"Mr. Lanigan," Trussel said. "First, you've asked us to reduce the charges from capital murder to destroying a dead body." People were surprised. Destroying a dead body? Parrish explained the recent developments in the case.

"Next, it's been suggested that this court should accept a plea of guilty to the charge of destroying a dead body. Mr. Parrish?" And Parrish told the story of Clovis.

"What's your plea, Mr. Lanigan?" the Judge asked.

"Guilty," Patrick said, firmly but with no pride.

"Does the state have a recommended punishment?"

Parrish walked to his table, looked through his notes, and returned to the Judge's desk. "Yes, Your Honor. I have a letter from Ms. Deena Postell of Meridian, Mississippi. She's a grandchild of Clovis Goodman." He handed a copy to Trussel. "In the letter, Ms. Postell asks this court not to punish Mr. Lanigan for burning her grandfather's dead body. He's been dead for over four years, and the family doesn't want any more suffering. So, the state recommends a punishment of twelve months in jail. However, this punishment can be dropped because of Mr. Lanigan's good behavior. We also recommend that he pay 5,000 dollars and all court costs."

"Mr. Lanigan, do you agree?" Trussel asked.

"Yes, Your Honor," Patrick said, unable to lift his head.

"Then I order you to make this payment within one week. Anything further?" Both lawyers quietly said no, and he closed the hearing.

Patrick exited quickly. He was anxious to leave, but he waited in Karl's office until it was dark and all the people had left. At seven o'clock, he said goodbye to Karl and thanked him for his friendship and help.

Sandy drove Patrick out of Biloxi to New Orleans. Using Sandy's car phone, Patrick called Eva. It was 3 A.M. in London, but she answered quickly.

"Eva, it's me," he said. "Yes, I'm fine. I've never felt better. And you?" He listened for a long time, his eyes closed, his head leaning back. Then he said, "I'll meet you in Aix, at the Hotel Gallici, on Sunday. I love you. I'll call you in a few hours."

They drove into Louisiana in silence. Then Sandy said, "I had a very interesting visitor this afternoon."

"Really, who?"

"Jack Stephano. He visited me at the hotel. He said he was sorry his boys injured you so much when they caught you. He told me about the person in Brazil who gave him information about you and about the Pluto Group. And he asked me directly if Eva sold the information. He's curious, because he found his man but didn't get the money."

"For the last three years, I've been chased in my sleep by a hundred men. All of them were hired by Jack Stephano. I finally got tired of it, Sandy. I gave up. Disappearing is an adventure until you learn that someone's trying to find you and is watching everything you do. I stole too much money, Sandy. They had to come after me. When I learned they were already in Brazil, I knew the end would come. So I decided to do it my way, not theirs."

Patrick breathed heavily, looked out the window, and tried to organize his thoughts. "The rewards were my idea, Sandy. Eva flew to Atlanta, where she met the Pluto Group. We paid them, and we gave Stephano information."

Sandy turned slowly, his mouth open. "You're lying," he said. "I know you're lying."

"No. We collected 1,150,000 dollars from Stephano. It's hidden now, probably in Switzerland with the rest of it."

"You don't know where it is?"

"She's been taking care of it. I'll find out when I see her."

Sandy was too shocked to say anything else. Patrick continued, "I knew they'd capture me, and I knew they'd try to make me talk. But I didn't know this would happen." He pointed to the rope mark above his left ankle. "They almost killed me. I finally gave up and told them about Eva. By then, she was gone, and so was the money."

"They almost killed you," Sandy said.

"That's true. But two hours after I was captured, Eva called Cutter in Biloxi, and he called the FBI in Washington. That's what saved my life. Stephano couldn't kill me because the FBI knew about it."

Sandy wanted to stop the car, get out, and scream. "You were a fool if you let them catch you."

"Oh, really? Didn't I just walk out of the courtroom a free man? Didn't I just talk with the woman I love dearly, a woman who's keeping a small fortune for me? The past is finally gone, Sandy. Don't you understand? There's no one looking for me anymore."

Sandy took him to his mother's house and drove away. In the morning, Patrick woke up smiling. His life of hiding was over. He and his mother talked, drove around the city, and did some shopping. Then Patrick went to the airport. He flew to Atlanta and from there to Nice, France.

He'd last seen Eva a month earlier, in Rio. She'd almost persuaded him to run and hide again, but he was tired of running. They'd said goodbye near her apartment. He'd kissed her and walked away, leaving her crying. He flew back to Ponta Pora and began waiting.

♦

On Sunday, when the train from Nice arrived in Aix, Patrick took a taxi to the Hotel Gallici. She'd reserved a room in both names, Eva Miranda and Patrick Lanigan, but she hadn't arrived yet, the clerk informed him.

He went to the room, unpacked, and fell asleep, dreaming of her. When he woke up, he went for a walk. Maybe they'd live here. They'd stay here for a week or so, then go back to Rio, but maybe Rio wouldn't be home. Feeling free, Patrick wanted to live everywhere, to experience different cultures, to learn different languages.

He refused to worry. He waited until dark, and then walked slowly back to the hotel. She wasn't there, and there was no message. He called the hotel in London and was informed that she'd left yesterday. He called her father. She was in London, Paulo said. He would say nothing more.

Patrick waited two hours and then called Sandy. "She's missing," he said, now frightened. Sandy hadn't heard from her.

Patrick stayed in Aix for two days, walking, calling Sandy and Paulo. Alone in his room, he cried from a broken heart. He drank too much alcohol. On the third day he left, asking a clerk to keep an envelope at the desk for Ms. Miranda if she arrived.

He flew to Rio. He wasn't sure why. She was too smart to go to Rio. Patrick had taught her too well how to disappear. No one would find Eva, unless she wanted them to.

He visited Paulo and told him the whole story, leaving him crying. He stayed in small hotels close to her apartment. Now he was the hunter, not the hunted, and a desperate one. He was almost out of money. Eventually, he called Sandy and asked to borrow 5,000 dollars. Sandy quickly agreed.

He gave up after a month, and returned to Ponta Pora. He could live in a country he loved, in a pleasant little town he also loved. Where else could he go? His journey was over. His past was finally closed.

Surely, some day she would find him.

ACTIVITIES

Chapters 1–3

Before you read

1 Are you familiar with Grisham's novels, and movies based on his novels? What kind of stories are they? Who are the heroes? Do you enjoy them? Why (not)?

2 Find these words in your dictionary. They are all in the story. Match each word with the best word below. What is the connection?

agent   arrest   fax   investigate   needle   torture

   a prisoner   **b** document   **c** drugs

   d detective   **e** criminal   **f** secret

3 Find these words in your dictionary. Use them to complete the sentences.

account   case   client   indict   release   wire

   a Please . . . . . the money to my Swiss bank . . . . . .

   b There isn't enough evidence to . . . . . Mr. Morrison for murder. We'll have to . . . . . him.

   c The . . . . . against the lawyer's . . . . . was weak.

After you read

4 How do you think Stephano's men found Patrick?

5 How are the following people connected?

   a Guy, Stephano, and Osmar

   b Patrick and Eva

   c Stephano, Jaynes, and Patrick

   d Aricia, Stephano and Patrick

6 Imagine that Patrick is able to telephone Eva from Puerto Rico. With a partner, act out their conversation.

Chapters 4–6

Before you read

7 Answer the questions. Find the words in *italics* in your dictionary.

   a Do you deny or refuse an *allegation*?

   b Is your *attorney* a doctor or a lawyer?

c Are *charges* made for or against a person?

d Do people get a *divorce* from their husband or their employer?

e If you *drop* the subject, do you continue or stop talking about it?

f Is *evidence* fact or opinion?

g Do you *file* a reward or a complaint?

h Is a *lawsuit* filed by the police or an individual?

i Are the *press* reporters or politicians?

j Do you *sue* someone for injuring you or helping you?

8 Does your country have a *death penalty*? If so, for what crimes? What do you think of this form of punishment?

After you read

9 Who:

  a is worried about Patrick?

  b isn't happy to know that Patrick is alive?

  c is going crazy?

  d is Patrick's old friend?

  e wants to indict Patrick for murder?

10 How do you feel about the behavior of :

  a Patrick?   **b** Eva?   **c** Sandy?   **d** Stephano?

Chapters 7–9

Before you read

11 Find these words in your dictionary. Use them to complete the sentences.

  bug cabin defendant hearing plea settlement

  a At his ..... the ..... said he didn't commit the crime. His ..... was "not guilty."

  b They went to a small ..... in the country and talked privately. They didn't know that there was a ..... in the room.

  c Several days after their disagreement, the managers and employees reached a ......

12 Discuss these questions.

  a Why does Stephano agree to talk to the FBI?

  b How will Patrick get what he wants in the divorce?

After you read

13 Why are these important in the story?

   a Patrick's shoe   **b** photographs   **c** a beard
   d a DNA test   **e** a boat   **f** a reward

14 Discuss these questions.

   a Patrick doesn't dress well for his hearing. Why not?
   b Why are so many people interested in Patrick's story?

Chapters 10–12

Before you read

15 Do you have *senators* in your country? Find the word in your dictionary. What do they do? If not, what do you have instead?

16 Patrick talks about the car crash. How do you think he felt after the crash?

After you read

17 What have you learned about how Patrick was found?

18 Who says these words? Why do you think the statements are important?

   a "You're safe now, Patrick."
   b "I guess it sounds romantic, doesn't it? Disappearing and becoming somebody new."
   c "And I'm supposed to change all my plans . . ."
   d "Their client . . . was ready to tell us everything."
   e "But he really needed a friend."
   f "It's all about money."

Chapters 13–15

Before you read

19 Patrick says he has another life to live. What kind of life do you think that is? Do you think he will live that life?

20 What do you think will happen to:

   a Eva?   **c** Aricia?
   b Stephano?   **d** Bogan and Vitrano?

After you read

21 Discuss these questions.

  a Patrick's appearance is different every time he goes to the courthouse. Why? Describe these differences.

  b Why is his behavior different when he goes in front of the grand jury and for his final hearing?

22 How do you feel about Patrick, Eva, Sandy, and Stephano now? Have your feelings changed? If so, how?

Writing

23 You are Eva. Write a letter to Patrick. Explain why you did not meet him. Tell him your future plans.

24 You are Patrick. Write a letter to Sandy, a year after returning to Ponta Pora. Explain how you feel now and your hopes for the future.

25 Do you think Patrick is a good or bad person? Give your reasons.

26 Which of the people in the story do you dislike most? Give your reasons.

27 Grisham says that in *The Partner* he wanted "to show that with money you can buy your way out of trouble." Is it right for people to be able to do this? Is it usual? Write about experiences you have read or heard about.

28 If you could disappear and begin a new life, where would you go? Describe your new life.

Answers for the Activities in this book are published in our free resource packs for teachers, the Penguin Readers Factsheets, or available on a separate sheet. Please write to your local Pearson Education office or to: Marketing Department, Penguin Longman Publishing, 5 Bentinck Street, London W1M 5RN.

BESTSELLING
PENGUIN READERS

AT LEVEL 5

The Body

The Firm

Four Weddings and a Funeral

The Great Gatsby

Jane Eyre

The Pelican Brief

The Prisoner of Zenda

Rebecca

Tales from Shakespeare

Taste and Other Tales

A Time to Kill

Wuthering Heights

www.pen   com

THE BEST WEBSITES FOR STUDENTS OF ENGLISH!

www.penguinreaders.com

Where the world of Penguin Readers comes to life

- Fully searchable on-line catalogue
- Downloadable resource materials
- First ever on-line Penguin Reader!
- New competition each month!

www.penguindossiers.com

Up-to-the-minute website providing articles for free!

- Articles about your favourite stars, blockbuster movies and big sports events!
- Written in simple English with fun activities!

CHECK THEM OUT!